Writers of Wales

GW00645300

Editors
MEIC STEPHENS   R. BRINLEY JONES

Don Dale-Jones

RAYMOND GARLICK

University of Wales Press

Cardiff 1996

I

Charles Whitmill became controller of the LMS railway between Chester and Holyhead during the first decade of the twentieth century, when his wife, Kate, was advised that seaside air would be good for her health. They lived in a large house in the middle of the village of Degannwy. In the early thirties, Kate's sister, Ellen, and her husband retired to the same village, and every year, sometimes twice a year, their grandson would come to them, from the new but to him depressing suburb of North Harrow, for his holidays. Crippled early in life, this impressionable boy looked on Gwynedd and Ynys Môn as a paradise. He was particularly struck, on visits to Bangor, by the *sombre splendour of the line of university buildings rising against the sky* ('A Small Boy in the Thirties, III', PLANET 104), and began to dream of becoming a student there, of spending a whole life, not just its holidays, in the *August Country*. He did not tell his parents of this fantasy, but when he grew up, he realized it. He became a fine poet, a gifted teacher and editor, a champion and reconciler of the two literatures of Wales. Of the second, the Anglo-Welsh, he was, if not the Messiah, then certainly the Saint Paul.

Raymond Garlick was born on 21 September 1926, in Harlesden, north-west London, the elder of the two sons of William and Elfreda Garlick. His father had served as a machine-gunner in France during the war of 1914–18 and been wounded and gassed. A beautifully mannered, generous, mild man with, nevertheless, a quiet authority (he is portrayed in 'The Visit'), he never talked about these experiences. Freda (as she was known) was the youngest daughter of William Alfred Beere, a tea-merchant in the City, and his wife, Alice, a woman of strong and serene character. She herself was formidable, with *strong views on everything, including her elder son*, though she was generous and compassionate. At the time of Raymond's birth they were living in the downstairs half of the home of the paternal grandparents, William and Ellen, and his father was employed by the National Bank as a clerk, a job that he found extremely uncongenial.

So far as I know, all my relatives on both sides were English, severely Nonconformist by religion, clerks, small tradesmen, artisans, by occupation. They were, in short, direct inheritors of the Puritan/Parliamentarian English tradition going back to the Civil War of the 17th Century – and earlier, to the Puritans whom Shakespeare disliked and mocked.

('A Small Boy in the Thirties, I', PLANET 102)

The Garlicks originated from Long Buckby, in Northamptonshire, and the Beeres from the village of Blagdon in Somerset. William Garlick kept a boot and shoe shop, repairing the shoes himself. The poet remembers him as *a red-pippin-cheeked little old man* smoking a pipe (PLANET 104). He had a fine tenor voice, as did his son, and Ellen sang well enough to have performed at Notre Dame in Paris with a visiting choir. William, Elfreda and their son continued to live with William's parents until they retired to Degannwy in 1930, then moved to a home of their own in a new estate on the edge of North Harrow where their second son, Julian, was born in 1933. William Alfred and Alice Beere lived nearby. Raymond Garlick retains vivid memories of them:

2

Alice Beere . . . was small in stature but immensely influential in her family circle. Calm, gentle, of great sweetness of character, dressed always in Victorian style, in lilacs and greys, she sat in her chair like a kind of Nonconformist abbess (as in the poem, 'Etching') quietly exerting almost absolute authority over her large husband and her formidable daughters.

(PLANET 104)

With William Alfred, he was to develop a close relationship. This grandfather was

large, moustached, rather grand in his dark overcoat with its velvet lapels and the rosebud that he always wore in his buttonhole

but he *deferred to my grandmother in everything*. His business was in Mincing Lane, and he never retired from it, continuing, until his death, to commute daily by train.

From the Harlesden period Raymond Garlick retains only scattered memories:

a hand-pushed milk-cart with a great brass churn into which a measure was dipped and the milk ladled out into one's jug; a man with a tray on his head, ringing a bell and calling 'Muffins'; a knock on the door and my mother looking out from behind the curtains . . . and refusing to answer – because it was gypsies selling clothes-pegs; being made (in the same room) to eat butter and sugar as a remedy for croup; the gift of a silk handkerchief which had belonged to someone recently deceased, rejected with repugnance on that account, and because of a distaste for its feel and texture . . .

('A Small Boy in the Thirties, II', PLANET 103)

– but its conclusion marked the end of carefree childhood.

3

He spent the year 1930–31 in hospitals, recovering from a crippling illness simply referred to at the time as septicaemia. Hospital was:

a place of terror . . . too much was visible. It is not good for small children to see death and suffering, or the theatres and technology of surgery to which they are to be submitted . . . few adults without children of their own are at ease in speaking to them. Most resort to facetiousness, a mode of speech bewildering to the small child. 'We're off to the theatre this afternoon', a nurse said to me archly. As, later in the day, I was once again wheeled (fully conscious) into the blazing operating room, with its glittering ranks of instruments, my last thought was how cruelly I had been deceived. Pain and infection too, in those pre-antibiotic days, were much more widespread. The food was dreadful, and I have been a lifelong vegetarian ever since. Perhaps the supreme failure of imagination lay in the fact that the natural source of comfort and courage at such a time, parents and relatives, were thought to have an upsetting effect upon sick children, so visiting was limited to once a fortnight, if not indeed once a month. I more or less forgot my poor parents, and I suppose I must have been almost as much a stranger to them when I was eventually discharged, for I spoke pure Cockney. (PLANET 103)

I have quoted at some length because this experience initiated a process of detachment from his parents which would be increased by the events of the war years and in part explains the poet's eventual severing of his roots in England in favour of new ones in Wales. Severe disability, with recurrent physical pain, will make a character or break it. Outside the home, particularly in school, and particularly at a time when public attitudes were crude and often cruel, the victim is constantly faced with emotional and physical problems. Raymond Garlick himself feels that those who survive are liable to be assertive to the point of rudeness and, having been all their lives inevitably self-preoccupied, may find it difficult to form close relationships. Poems such as 'Biographical Note', first published in THE WELSH-SPEAKING SEA (1954), deal specifically with the problem:

> *I live in a rakish body framed*
> *about a spine like a buckled spire*
>
> *or twisted spring, my uncurled crown of thorn . . .*
>
> > *to poise and pin*
>
> *a pattern on deformity, to voice*
> *the un-neat not-known: this is the hot desire*
> *locked in my knotted limbs and body's vice.*
> *And thus I am, and thus you see me now:*
> *a hustings for a heart wrapped in a wrack*
> *lusting for words to shape itself anew.*

This problem lies at the centre of the poet's wrestle to make order out of a chaos of words and experience and explains also his refusal, in shop, classroom, literary argument or life itself, to be passed over or put down.

Physical recovery was slow: crutches, then one crutch, finally just the walking-stick which has been essential ever since. Able to take a close interest again in his surroundings, he found that the new house on the new estate at the edge of countryside, a delight to his parents, was a disappointment to him. He did not like the felling of trees, the destruction, by rapidly extending suburbia, of fields, ponds and woodland:

it represented boredom, dullness, rootlessness. Nothing I saw around me, apart from a few great elms still unfelled, was older than myself. As the name of the place testified, it existed only as a compass reference in relation to somewhere else. The acres of pink semi-detached houses on their well laid-out roads, with grass verges and flowering trees, seemed a desert . . .

(PLANET 102)

A significant pleasure was walking to Pinner, still recognizably a village, where his parents' strongly anti-Catholic prejudices probably encouraged his nervous exploration of the dark interior of the Roman Catholic church with its dimly burning red lights and strong smell of incense.

His primary education had begun and, in the absence of the paternal grandparents in Degannwy, he spent much time with the Beeres. He used to meet his grandfather at the station, where he would sometimes see the *Royal Scot* or the blue and silver *Coronation Scot* thunder by. 'The Words in My Life' (ANGLO-WELSH REVIEW 13, 31) opens with a vivid memory of this time:

'The Snark', said my grandfather – inserting the ferrule of his umbrella, with great presence of mind, between the closing doors of the Bakerloo train – 'The Snark' was a Boojum, you see.' The doors grumbled open again, and with great dignity my grandfather entered and, like the Boojum in question, 'suddenly vanished away' in the direction of Baker Street.

The small boy would accompany the old man home to sit with him while he ate his dinner. He was affectionate and talked interestingly about people, books and ideas. He is commemorated in the poem, 'The Commuter', and summed up in 'A Small Boy in the Thirties, III':

6

his humour, individually, integrity; his genial puritanism (he was a Nonconformist lay-preacher, and a teetotaller constantly amused by his incongruous surname); his direct descent from those Anabaptist merchants of Tudor London, through the Parliamentarian Dissenters of the Civil War period, to the moderately radical, eminently civilized, admired views of Tony Benn . . . their inheritor today, of whom (he) would have warmly approved . . .

which goes on to speak of literary, verbal and orthographic influences:

My grandfather's written English was finely inscribed, out of reverence for the word – the shape as well as the sound of thought. His spoken English was flavoured with the warm burr of the West Country from which he came. He would sit in his great padded and winged armchair, and – riding above the soft singing of the gas-fire – his voice would rejoice in Lord Macaulay's LAYS OF ANCIENT ROME, *Jerome K. Jerome's* THREE MEN IN A BOAT, *but above all in the writings of Lewis Carroll.*

and associates him with Raymond Garlick's perception of the colours of words (see, for example, 'Vowels' in LANDSCAPE AND FIGURES, 1964). It was William Alfred Beere, with his recitations of 'Jabberwocky' and 'The Walrus and the Carpenter', who made poetry a part of everyday life, an experience built on at primary school with Whittier's 'Barbara Frietchie', Southey's 'Inchcape Rock' and, supremely, Longfellow's 'Hiawatha'.

It was common, and entirely safe, before and for some years after the Second World War, for suburban children to travel alone into the city. Throughout the thirties, the major (though not the more significant) part of Raymond Garlick's experience was London experience. He recalls standing with his parents at the foot of the Duke of York's Steps in the Mall:

to see the king-emperor George V ride by, followed by his four sons, all on horseback, to the Trooping of the Colour. Behind us, at the top of the steps, above the first great house in the terrace to the left, a swastika flag flapped on what was then the embassy of Nazi Germany . . . (PLANET 102)

and, a sight which he never forgot and which played its part in determining his opinions for the rest of his life:

Late one summer afternoon I was walking along the Mall, on the St James's Park side, with my aunt [his mother's eldest sister, who never married and is the subject of the poem 'Miss Beatrice'] *when a series of huge motor-cars began drawing up along the whole length of the very wide pavement. Out of them got chauffeurs, who set up folding camp-stools and then served champagne to the glittering creatures who sat down there. All wore court dress, the women in white, with ostrich plumes, tiaras and jewels, the men with gold lace on their coats, and the sashes, ribbons, crosses and stars of orders. They chatted quietly, indifferent to passers-by, sipped their champagne, and at a given signal re-entered their cars and were driven down the Mall. My aunt said it was the occasion of a levée . . .*
(PLANET 102)

Home experience such as pictures in the DAILY MIRROR of Mussolini (*a clowning oaf*) and Hitler (*a sinister version of Charlie Chaplin*), of the exiled Haile Selassie and of Gandhi, one of an elderly, bearded Jew being beaten up and Count von Galen, Bishop of Münster, defying the Stormtroopers in his cathedral, and the sight of humbled, polite ex-servicemen begging at the door combined to lay the foundations of a republican radicalism. There were less contentious mind-broadening experiences – visits to the South Kensington museums, tea and toast in the Lyons teashops and Corner Houses, *the ordinary person's Savoy or Ritz*, an illustrated article on Renoir in the PICTURE POST, which provided *the first astonishing data on the female form.*

Knowledge of Wales began with convalescence at Degannwy, and, throughout the thirties, contrasted with and started to raise questions about the validity of the London experience. Raymond Garlick came to perceive North Harrow as:

a desert in which none of the things which I was obscurely aware were going to be important to me – history, the past, art, books, nature, the countryside, Europe – had any place . . . its values – apart from tennis and bridge – were political chauvinism, religious sectarianism, xenophobia, with an inbuilt tendency to anti-semitism, and a sympathy among some for the British Union of Fascists . . . (PLANET 102)

but the particular 'myth' of Wales, central to all of his writing, could not have been realized without it. The perception, instinctive at first, of a contrast of cultures, enabled him to discover in Wales a European tradition – *a culture of peace, of the intellect and the arts* (ARTISTS IN WALES, 2) long abandoned by imperialist England. What strikes one most forcibly about Raymond Garlick's life is the way in which the man's unpleasant and potentially tragic experiences have so often been good fortune for the artist.

The early journeys to Degannwy were made by train via Rugby, Stafford, Crewe and Chester:

After Chester there was the heightened consciousness of entering Wales, the frequent stops along the northern coast, the sea on the right, hills rising to the left, and – as we neared our destination – a magnificence of mountains. Degannwy station, its outer wall washed by the sea, with the great whale-back of Mynydd Conwy opposite, the glimpsed towers of Castell Conwy, and far beyond that the distinctive outline of Moel Siabod, was an exciting place to get out at. (PLANET 104)

The child became closely acquainted with the Welsh countryside. His grandparents' home backed onto open land fragrant with meadowsweet, wild thyme, clover and vetch. Behind the nearby church rose the Vardre,

the first hill I climbed, thus signalling some sort of return to normal mobility . . . I played . . . among the remains of a site associated with both Maelgwyn Gwynedd and Llywelyn Fawr. Here in 1966 was found 'The Stone Face' now in the National Museum, which is the subject of Harri Webb's fine poem . . .
(PLANET 104)

Many years later he would recall his feelings in 'August Country':

> *That's what Wales was, for me*
> *as a child: an Edward Thomas land*
> *of holidays, the blood's tree*
> *warm with nightingales; the span of sand*
> *a fortnight in the year's infinity.*

Although his great-aunt, uncle and grandparents were English in-comers, they committed themselves to Wales. Ellen Garlick learned to sing in Welsh; Charles Whitmill became alderman and mayor of Conwy; his only daughter became a Jones by marriage and all the descendants are native Welsh-speakers. At a time when the hinterland of Gwynedd and Ynys Môn was intensely Welsh-speaking, the boy mixed naturally with its inhabitants. His first Welsh word was *Rhybudd*, from the level-crossing gates through which he passed on his way to the sea; the only other place where, at that time, Welsh was to be seen in public was on chapel notice-boards.

Welsh associations, powerful in memory because they evoked the freedoms of holiday time, began to accumulate. Late one night in 1935 he was taken to the bedroom window to see Conwy Bridge illuminated in honour of George V's jubilee. There were trips in the paddle-steamer up the then navigable Conwy river to Trefriw, bathing from Anglesey beaches almost deserted even in August:

What a limited experience of Wales gave to this small boy in the Thirties was the glimmering of an idea that there was somewhere in these Islands where life need not be as boring, bland, restricting, characterless, unvaried, rootless, as it was in London suburbia. (PLANET 104)

Back home, shortly before the happiness of a humane primary school gave way to the sterner regime of Harrow Boys' County School, there was information from an older boy about

what are somewhat hyperbolically called the facts of life (so startling and totally unanticipated that I almost fell out of a tree with surprise)

and a first *powerful experience of the numinous* while walking in woodland one beautiful Sunday morning.

11

He was not destined to remain long enough at the County School to recover from a first-day experience which, for him, epitomized its atmosphere:

The form-master, an amiable and not insensitive man, worked down the list of his new charges and invented a nickname for each – one of the many ways in which the county schools (later to be called grammar schools) aped the so-called public schools. The tag attached to my own name highlighted disability, the rationale no doubt being that it was better to face facts and come to terms with the obvious. It did not, however, enable him to foresee and forestall the first approaching contretemps. A quarter of an hour later we were marched into the vast assembly hall, where from the platform the granite-faced headmaster, swathed in black silk, curtly instructed the assembly to sit – meaning, of course, cross-legged on the floor. They did so, and (it being physically impossible for me) I alone remained standing in that ocean of hundreds of seated boys. Understandably, this was taken to imply rebelliousness or stupidity. An appalled silence ensued, followed by a further admonition barked at 'That boy'. Awed and confused by the whole situation, I could say and do nothing. (PLANET 103)

Shortly after the outbreak of war, while his younger brother remained in London with their parents, he was sent to live with his father's cousin and her *warmly eccentric husband, a master-baker and confectioner . . . in business in Degannwy.* There, in daily contact with the Welsh-speaking employees, he learned his first Welsh phrase, *Cymru am byth*, from tins of toffee on sale in the shop. He entered the John Bright County School, Llandudno, and found it in all ways better than Harrow *with its relaxed and civilized order, its warm eccentricities, its brilliant teaching.*

Charles Jones, his English teacher, extended the process begun by William Alfred Beere and

12

developed by a first-class primary education. Raymond Garlick retains vivid memories of him:

as he leant against the corner of a fireplace, his arms folded under a voluminous and tattered gown . . . I sometimes privately saw [him] as an eagle-nosed Blackfoot chieftain, and sometimes as a wise but predatory and swooping owl.
('Inspiration and Perspiration', POETRY WALES, 24, 1, 1988)

Of the GOLDEN TREASURY selection for the Central Welsh Board examination in 1942, he remembers Goldsmith's 'The Deserted Village', Burns's 'Tam O'Shanter', Gray's 'Elegy' and Browning's 'Abt Vogler' and 'A Death in the Desert'. What would later be recognized as the impulse to become a writer was strengthened by the perspicacity of a teacher of French who lent him, at the age of fourteen, Axel Munthe's THE STORY OF SAN MICHELE. At the age of fifteen and a half, inevitably:

came the piercing and appalled realization that the whole of life was to be lived in a crippled mode: that symmetry of physique, physical achievement, grace and ease of movement, were forever unattainable . . . For years the recollection of that wretched adolescent was a matter of shame . . . some kind of breakdown ensued. With the wisdom of gifted teachers, Charles Jones and others issued kindly instructions not to attend school any more, to go and lie on the beach every day, simply to come in when there was an examination paper to sit. This humane advice resulted . . . in a return to mental stability, and the incidental gain of a matriculation certificate. (Ibid.)

Nobody on either side of the Garlick family had ever attended university. The assumption was that you left school as soon as it was permitted, to earn your own living and contribute to that of the family. As

13

soon, therefore, as he had matriculated, Raymond Garlick was recalled to London and sent to work in the laboratories of the Kodak factory in Wealdstone. Although not unhappy there, he left after six months for the Community of the Resurrection's hostel in Leeds, having felt a call to the Anglican priesthood.

Aspirant ordinands were required to take a BA at the University of Leeds before receiving theological instruction at Mirfield. His matriculation had not included Latin, then a condition of university entrance, so his first task was to acquire, before the summer examinations, sufficient proficiency to obtain a pass. Having done so, in October he became a student at the university, following courses in Ancient History, Latin and the Philosophy and History of Religion. In the examinations of the following year, however, his Latin proved inadequate and he was failed – but this hardly signified, for he realized he had no vocation.

It had been eclipsed by the dream, still concealed from his parents, of reading English at Bangor. Convinced now that this must be his way forward, he sought means of obtaining entrance and financing a course which would for him be a four-year one. There was no question of parental contribution: they had not the resources and could not, in any case, approve. A consideration in his favour was that, this being 1944, the number of students at university was small. His home county, Middlesex, was prepared to offer him a loan for the first year, and the Bangor authorities accepted his year at Leeds as an entry qualification. Fees were lower in Wales, but he would have to win university awards to survive. October 1944 found him, scarcely at first able to believe it, in his Intermediate year, studying Latin, English, Philosophy and History:

the icy buildings at Bangor – dimly lit, staircases and open-air corridors swept by storms of rain and wind, the leaded windows of the lecture-rooms pounded by gales – were echoing and largely empty places, inhabited only by a handful of elderly academics and medically-unfit students. In consequence a naïve 18 year-old undergraduate like myself had passing acquaintance with men of the greatest distinction: Sir Emrys Evans, translator into Welsh of Plato's REPUBLIC*; Sir Ifor Williams, a little hunched owl, the great scholar of the* GODODDIN*; Sir John Edward Lloyd, the Welsh medieval historian.*

('Portfolio', PLANET 107, October 1994)

In spite of being naïve and shy, and of having grown up in a tradition distrustful of foreigners, the undergraduate made a wide range of friends. He was helped in this by his association, during the months before term began, with the Sachs family, exiles from Berlin, who then lived near his London home. They gave him access to a *metropolitan European culture of art and ideas* ('Some Painters', PLANET 108) and began his education in visual art.

He was impressed by the teaching of R. T. Jenkins and Hywel D. Lewis. A pacifist, he naturally attended meetings of the group which included Lady Artemus Jones, Dr Thomas Parry (whom he would meet many years later, as *Sir* Thomas Parry, in the Literature Committee of the Welsh Arts Council) and G. O. Williams, later Archbishop of Wales. His connection with OMNIBUS, the student magazine, would be useful later, but his most important, prophetic and peculiar contact was with:

Louis Soeterboek, who under the name Louis Olav Leroi

15

published two very slim but hardback volumes of poetry in English . . . and a short novel in Welsh entitled BENEDICT GYMRO. *He was a good deal older than I was, and wore the Khaki uniform of the army of the Kingdom of the Netherlands, though with his thick-lensed spectacles and moustacheless beard a more unsoldierly soldier is difficult to imagine.* (PLANET 107)

As we have seen, Raymond Garlick had, from an early age, been responsive to poetry, but before the meeting with Soeterboek it had never occurred to him to write any. D. H. Lawrence, in a 'Note' to his COLLECTED POEMS, recalled that

The first poems I ever wrote, if poems they were, was [sic] *when I was nineteen: now twenty-three years ago. I remember perfectly the Sunday afternoon when I perpetrated those first two pieces: 'To Guelder-Roses' and 'To Campions' . . . Any young lady might have written them and been pleased with them . . .*

Recalling, about fifty years after the event, his own *appalling début*, Raymond Garlick would be even more scornful. Much less conventional than Lawrence's, it is worth recalling in his own words:

For me the immediate external agency which started off the writing of verse is easy to place, and far from mysterious. It was a request from . . . Louis Soeterboek, for some poems for the College magazine. The request was so expressed as to imply that all literate persons wrote poetry as a matter of course, that naturally one had some at the ready. Out of sheer pique I went back to my lodgings and wrote something . . .

('Inspiration and Perspiration')

The first poem to appear in a literary magazine was 'Lines on THE PRAYING HANDS by Albrecht Dürer'

(THE POETRY REVIEW, Vol. XXXVII, 1946) and in December 1946 he shared the privately printed POEMS MCMXLVII with Soeterboek (thirteen and twelve pieces respectively). Even this small and very early collection has points of interest: its mixture of sonnets and lyrics is characteristic, as is its preoccupation with nature, art and music; its 'Sonnet: John Donne' (*He was a tower of flame, a pealing storm*) is prophetic. Even at this stage Raymond Garlick appeared to know instinctively where and how to secure publication: he managed to ease his finances by placing some of his best essays (the accomplished 'Milton and Dante' for example) in the POETRY REVIEW and by reviewing for the BRITISH WEEKLY. Three guineas was a significant sum in those days.

Poetry and art were united in his friendship with Brenda Chamberlain which began with an invitation to meet another Dutchman, Louis Eveleens, at the home of Lady Artemus Jones in Upper Bangor. Eveleens was staying with Brenda Chamberlain, thirty-three years of age at the time and, following her separation from John Petts in 1943, living on at their cottage, Tŷ'r Mynydd, on the mountainside a mile or two from Llanllechid. When she decided to settle on Ynys Enlli, the studio half of Tŷ'r Mynydd was rented to Raymond Garlick for £13 a year and it remained his home until he moved to Pembroke Dock in 1949:

This was Brenda's most lasting influence on my life – the implied challenge of her own vigorous, independent life-style. No greater contrast can be imagined than between my London suburban home and Tŷ'r Mynydd. The door opened into the main room with its huge open hearth, slate floor, beamed roof.

17

Off it was the small siambr *where I slept in winter, and above that – and reached by a ladder – the* lloft, *with a skylight, where I slept in summer. This meant that there was a spare room and visitors could come to stay – my brother, members of the Sachs family, fellow-students.* (PLANET 108)

Life in this isolated setting required self-dependence:

For a nervous, protected, disabled young man, the experiment of living alone, without electricity and plumbing, having to break the ice and carry water from the well, climb the mountainside in the snow in search of wood to drag home and cut: such a life presented itself as a necessary challenge. Its influence has been lasting. (ARTISTS IN WALES, 2, pp. 87–8)

The Welsh landscape and a growing knowledge of its history, the intellectual challenge of studying alongside students from Europe, the empire and, with the arrival of ex-service undergraduates, the rest of the world (including its batttlefields), a practical insight into art, association with Welsh writers in both languages and the developing poet's natural interest in their craft began, during the Bangor years (a *radiant experience*, he calls them, in the 1991 interview in POETRY WALES) the formation of an individual voice. In 1944 Keidrych Rhys's MODERN WELSH POETRY appeared:

It contained the work of 37 Anglo-Welsh poets, but its most immediate interest to me was that it contained work by Charles Davies, a senior lecturer in the English department . . . I don't think he was a very good poet, but to be taught by someone who was writing and publishing poems made poetry a significant and contemporary activity . . . ('Dock Leaves and Nettles')

The BBC Welsh Home Service has an honourable

place in the development of modern Anglo-Welsh poetry, along with the WESTERN MAIL of the pre- and immediately post-war period. A number of poets obtained early publication in the latter's 'Wales Day by Day' column, and, with A. G. Prys-Jones as a reviewer and broadcaster, their collections could be sure of perceptive and kindly notice. In that autumn of 1946, Raymond Garlick found himself, not without reservations, involved in the 35-minute broadcasts, 'Welsh Muse: Our Modern Poets' which went out on 23 October and 21 November. (The invitation came from Alun Llywelyn-Williams.) After an introduction by Keidrych Rhys, Pennar Davies commented on works by Rhys, Glyn Jones, Peter Hellings, Ken Etheridge, Lynette Roberts and R. S. Thomas and the poems were read by Raymond Garlick and his fellow-reader. For the next two years:

my closest . . . contacts with Anglo-Welsh writing were through Brenda Chamberlain . . . In College, in the Students' Union, I learned to recognize Emyr Humphreys – returned from the war with his first novel, THE LITTLE KINGDOM, already under his belt . . . I saw the Caseg press on which the beautiful broadsheets had been printed, and which had been the occasion of Alun Lewis's visit. There too I met Denys Val Baker, editor of THE CORNISH REVIEW – who, I seem to remember, came from Penmaenmawr. I believe Brenda contributed to THE CORNISH REVIEW – as she certainly did to LIFE AND LETTERS TODAY, edited by Robert Herring, one of the poets represented in Keidrych Rhys's anthology . . . Glyn Jones records . . . that in the thirties and forties Robert Herring's publication was regarded almost as a third Anglo-Welsh magazine, so encouraging was its editor towards us.

('Dock Leaves and Nettles')

There was also a book, *unpublished and unpublishable*, influenced by THE STORY OF SAN MICHELE, which

19

gave useful experience of sustained writing in prose.

The Welsh evening classes which, with his uncle and aunt, Raymond Garlick had attended at Llandudno in the early 1940s, helped him realize his desire to be a part of the *intensely and naturally Welsh and Welsh-speaking* atmosphere of Bangor. He became friends with Elin Hughes, who was studying Welsh, French and Philosophy. Her father worked for Trinity House and her mother came from a prosperous, farm-owning family. On both sides the family was Nonconformist, Welsh-speaking and deeply rooted in Anglesey. They lived at Holyhead, on the island beyond the island, next to a convent built by her grandfather and inhabited by cultivated French nuns whose mother-house was at Caen. Bilingual already, Elin had formed the habit of visiting the convent, where she soon became fluent in French. In adolescence, without objection from her parents, she had been received into the Roman Catholic Church. When, in 1945, the nuns visited the shattered town of Caen to re-establish contact, she went with them.

Raymond Garlick and Elin Hughes graduated in 1948 and were married shortly afterwards. He had been received into the Catholic Church on the evening before the ceremony. Although fiercely Welsh, to the point of intolerance, and an active Nationalist, she was by no means typically so, for her contact with the nuns of Holyhead and her visits to Caen had made her a francophile. Elin was to have an enormous influence on her husband. He had married Europe and Wales simultaneously, for she would not only give him insight into Welsh language and culture, but also inspire him with her enthusiasm for France. His first volume, POEMS FROM

THE MOUNTAIN-HOUSE, contains a poem based on a translation by his wife of a piece by Ceiriog.

With the responsibilities of marriage and the Middlesex loan to pay off within five years, he could not afford to take the PGCE (known in those days as the Diploma in Education). His final year had, however, included an anticipatory fortnight of lightly supervised teaching at Penygroes County School, which he had thoroughly enjoyed. Graduates were not, in any case, required to be trained, nor was the reputation of the Bangor department of education (like that of many university departments, then and for years to come) such as to inspire sacrifice. There was no question of a graduate's being unable to find employment as soon as he cared to look for it; with his second vocation confirmed, he took a post at an enlightened preparatory school in Bangor (boys and girls from six to twelve), to teach French. Fortunately, elementary French would suffice.

His colleagues were the wives of university professors, competent women of high intelligence, happy to find congenial employment. He learned a great deal from them and, as the appointment was for two terms only, and the children young, was able to make, without damage to himself or his pupils, those initial mistakes that even the most gifted young teachers cannot avoid. In April 1949 he was appointed by its new headmaster, Roland Mathias, to the staff of Pembroke Dock County School. (This was the first appointment Roland Mathias had made – Raymond Garlick maintains that he had wanted Glyn Jones but had been unable to attract him away from the post in Cardiff where, by not enjoying the work excessively, he was able to keep time and energy free for his writing.) There is delightful irony in Raymond Garlick's recollection that, *a solemn, ingenuous and callow young man*, at interview, he so far forgot that Mathias's verse had been represented in MODERN WELSH POETRY as to assert that he had *no time for all this Anglo-Welsh nonsense* ('On the Growing of DOCK LEAVES', PLANET 9).

The Pembroke Dock years, from April 1949 to September 1954, were to be crucial in a number of ways. There was a conscious confirmation of the commitment to Wales:

my plan of life took its second decisive step forward when I began as assistant English master at Pembroke Dock County School – and thus became a salary-earner, a taxpayer, a ratepayer, and elector in Wales: crucial elements in becoming rooted, belonging, becoming committed.

('Dock Leaves and Nettles')

More important was the emotional impact of the contrast between Gwynedd (mountainous, largely Welsh-speaking, a personal heartland as well as that of Wales) and South Pembrokeshire (flat, largely English-speaking, with Anglicized place-names which grated on his ear). It was heart, not head, which determined his acceptance of

a responsibility towards the culture and languages of the adopted country . . . a duty to defend it, and an obligation to cast one's vote . . . in what one judges to be its best interests.

('Choosing Wales', in DISCOVERING WELSHNESS, pp. 57–8)

There was the need to develop professional competence as a teacher of English to Welsh children. For a teacher who was also a poet, this involved learning a great deal about his subject, his poetic vocation, his pupils and himself. Working out the best way of teaching English developed awareness of the Anglo-Welsh tradition whose very existence he had joined the literary and academic establishments in denying.

The 'Dock Leaves Group' – through which he became, at the age of twenty-three, editor of the only Anglo-Welsh periodical in existence – would complete his education. Roland Mathias had brought together a disparate band, most of them university graduates, who met monthly to listen to, and discuss, a paper prepared by one of them – on Goethe, THE BACCHAE of Euripides, history, music, the visual arts. It was he who, tongue-in-cheek, suggested the title of the magazine in which they would publish their work and that of many others:

how important a role this whole experience played in my own life. Taking one's turn at preparing and delivering a paper, deciding upon and giving notice of its subject, concentrated the mind wonderfully, encouraged reading, thinking, researching.
('Dock Leaves and Nettles')

The editorship provided opportunities enjoyed by few young teachers. There were meetings in 1952 with Éamon de Valera and John Cowper Powys. Publishing 'Depopulation of the Hills' led to a lifelong friendship with R. S. Thomas; there were similar friendships with A. G. Prys-Jones and Glyn Jones and correspondence with Idris Davies, David Jones, Huw Menai, George Ewart Evans, Henry Treece and T. H. Jones. Even more important was contact with Welsh-medium writers: Saunders

Lewis, D. J. and Waldo Williams, and the writing, over a period of more than ten years, of a series of twenty-five editorials which developed his view of Anglo-Welsh writing and helped clarify important personal, national and literary issues. There were sacrifices too; he had to give up his MA dissertation on 'Chaucer and the Rhetoricians'.

His first volume of poetry, POEMS FROM THE MOUNTAIN-HOUSE, was published by the Fortune Press in 1950. He had taken the title from Brenda Chamberlain's cottage and some of the poems had appeared in the BRITISH WEEKLY, the POETRY REVIEW and ENGLISH and in the WESTERN MAIL. This was Holy Year for Roman Catholics, so he and Elin decided to extend a European experience begun with holidays in France and Spain in 1948 and 1949 by making the pilgrimage to Rome. They set off in July to walk and hitch-hike across England and France, staying at religious houses where free overnight accommodation was available for pilgrims. They reached Rome at midnight in company with a lorry-load of fruit-pickers from Florence, stayed for the three days for which free accommodation was available, then made their way home again. Including the Channel crossing, this formative experience had cost them £15.

In 1952 they adopted their first child, Iestyn. In 1953 Dylan Thomas, shortly before his death, came to Tenby to give a public reading of UNDER MILK WOOD. Meeting him for the first and only time, Raymond Garlick was impressed by his charm, humility and grace. The encounter inspired 'The Poet Reads his Play at Tenby' and the lyric elegy 'Poem for Dylan'. The much more formal elegy, 'Requiem for a Poet'

(DOCK LEAVES PAMPHLET, 1: 1954), is a tribute to the young Welsh poet, R. Aled Hughes. Later that year the same press published the twelve 'Poems from Pembrokeshire' (DOCK LEAVES PAMPHLET, 2) soon to be included in THE WELSH-SPEAKING SEA. Reviewing this collection, Glyn Jones wrote:

we have no longer to consider the work of a poet in the process of finding himself but of one who has attained an inner certainty and equipoise . . . found his subject matter, and developed an almost complete assurance of manner.

It was an equally important year for Raymond Garlick's work on the Anglo-Welsh tradition. The January–March issue of the DUBLIN MAGAZINE contained the article 'Anglo-Welsh Poetry from 1587 to 1800' and in the December issue of THE WELSH ANVIL (with 'Seventy Anglo-Welsh Poets') he nailed to the establishment's doors six general propositions supported by a detailed list beginning with Morris Kyffin (*c.* 1555–98).

He left Pembroke Dock for Ffestiniog County School in the summer of 1954. At Pembroke Dock he had felt that the town, badly bombed during the war, run down, desolate, was hardly a community at all, whereas the school, under the vigorous direction of Roland Mathias, was vibrant with life; Blaenau was the opposite – the school disappointing, the town visually thrilling, dramatic as the stage of a theatre, warmly human. He had returned to what he felt was the *real* Wales in order that his son should receive his education in a Welsh-speaking area and acquire the language naturally. Standing one day on a school staircase with an exciting view over the valley, he realized that he had achieved professional maturity

– never again would anything happen that he could not cope with instinctively.

He continued to edit what he had renamed the ANGLO-WELSH REVIEW and enjoyed a warm friendship with John Cowper Powys (1872–1963):

really coming to know him dated from the moment when, early in 1955, I encountered him and his life's companion, Phyllis Playter, in a torrential downpour on the main street of Blaenau Ffestiniog, and they told me that they had just bought a small cottage and were coming to live there . . . he was nearly eighty when I first met him. I always called him Mr Powys, and that is how I still think of him . . . though it would have been entirely acceptable for me to have called him John . . . There was nothing in the least distant or condescending, pompous or histrionic, about him: he was natural, open, spontaneous, warm, and beautifully mannered.

In appearance he was immensely distinguished – tall, spare, with a slight stoop, ascetic of feature, his head crowned with a mass of tight silver curls . . . The portrait head that Augustus John was to draw of him . . . is a good likeness and evokes his glowing vivacity, and yet there is something slightly feminine about it – which was wholly lacking in JCP . . . Whenever I greeted or left him I was conscious that the hand I took had clasped those of so many English and American writers who were illustrious names in the histories of literature . . . there was also the consciousness that the blood of two of the English poets whose work I most enjoyed, Donne and Cowper, flowed in the veins of that long bony hand.

('Mr Powys and Miss Playter', PLANET 110, April 1995)

Mr Powys would, between 1972 and 1995, be the subject of three memorable essays.

In 1955 Raymond Garlick decided to enter the *Semi-National* or London Eisteddfod because he noticed that its regulations permitted the *pryddest* to be composed in either Welsh or English. The subject was 'Y Ddinas' and an idea, stimulated by Blaenau, and a form (rhymed triplets), occurred to him. He gained enormous pleasure from the composition, feeling for the first time master of his craft, and the poem won him a chair and pushed his great friend, James Nicholas, into second place. Raymond Garlick was the first to concede that judgement between works on the same subject but in different languages could not be equitable and was happy to see the regulations altered for the following year. He was delighted, however, not to have missed the experience of being a chaired bard – unique, surely for an Englishman? The chair-winning poem formed the core of BLAENAU OBSERVED, his tribute to his new home, which was broadcast (BBC Welsh Home Service) on 14 June 1956 and printed, with a dedication to Powys, by the Dock Leaves Press in 1957. Throughout the fifties he kept up the engagement with radio broadcasting which had begun at Bangor, featuring, under the direction of Aneirin Talfan Davies (*probably the best friend the Anglo-Welsh had among writers in Welsh*), in programmes from Cardiff and Swansea and later, under that of Dyfnallt Morgan, from Bangor. He has written at some length about this in 'Dylan Thomas and Others' (PLANET 109).

It was in the late 1950s that he developed the beautiful italic handwriting that makes correspondence with him an aesthetic experience. Although it arose from a teacher's unhappiness about his untidy blackboard-style (and the inevitable effect on pupils' orthography), it was a further example of the pinning of a syntax on existence described in 'Biographical Note'. Of course he taught the same style to the children.

Although never entirely happy with the administration of the school, he had had no thoughts of leaving it, yet Christmas 1960 saw the family travelling through a blizzard to Harwich. From January 1961 he was on the staff of the International School at Eerde Castle in the Netherlands. Editing had been put behind him, but Wales had not: he retained a cottage in Llanffestiniog and the family, completed by the adoption of a daughter, Angharad, in 1958, returned each year for extended holidays.

What had happened was that the son of an acquaintance of Pembroke Dock days had left university without a degree. Employment being hard to find, he had eventually gone abroad, and his parents were bemused to learn that he was teaching in the Netherlands. They knew nothing whatever about the establishment with the strange name, and found it hard to believe that their son, with no obvious qualifications, could have obtained a teaching post. It was to Raymond Garlick, with his experience of foreign travel, that they turned, and in July 1960 he had visited the young man, found that there was nothing wrong, been shown around the school and met its principal and members of its hospitable staff. Eerde Castle and its estate of small farms, heathland and undulating forest four kilometres from the town of Ommen *was a place of extraordinary beauty, solitude and peace*, and the Dutch people whom he met extremely congenial. He noted these things, returned to Blaenau, and was astonished to receive, not long afterwards, an invitation to take over the teaching of English. No testimonials would be required and his wife fully supported the move, so he was able to leave the County School with minimum notice. He soon realized that, as so often half-instinctively, he had acted in the best interests of his art and life: Eerde was an important stimulus to poetry

because of the release it gave from editorship . . . from the advocacy of a model of Anglo-Welsh literature to which there then seemed no response, and from a profound disillusion with the British education system as embodied by the frustrations offered by one school in Wales.
('Fourth of May', ANGLO-WELSH REVIEW, No. 62, 1978)

This feeling and a recognition of the contrasting excellence of the International School led to a number of articles in the TIMES EDUCATIONAL SUPPLEMENT, EDUCATION and elsewhere.

The whole family was so happy at Eerde (Elin teaching mathematics and beginning her translations from Dutch into Welsh) that he began to think about Dutch citizenship. The culture of the Netherlands, like that of Wales, was one *of peace, of the intellect and the arts,* its sense of Europe typified for him by a Dutch Professor of Celtic, Marcia Draak, lecturing in Utrecht about the MABINOGI. Since THE WELSH-SPEAKING SEA, his poems had been appearing in a wider range of periodicals, and in 1964 the Merrythought Press published LANDSCAPES AND FIGURES, a rigorous selection of poems written between 1949 and 1963. By 1967, however, the family was ready to return home; he saw clear evidence of progress in Wales in the finding of a role for Anglo-Welsh literature and he had begun to feel the sense of a debt to repay. When a post at Trinity College,

Carmarthen, was advertised, offering not merely a return to a Welsh-speaking area but also the opportunity to advance, within education in Wales, his views about the importance of the Anglo-Welsh tradition, he applied for it, was accepted and, in September 1967, joined Wyn Binding's department.

If he had been happy in the Netherlands, he was supremely so at Trinity. The department was one in which members were encouraged to pursue their own specialisms while at the same time, through team-teaching, they shared those of colleagues. Its head was always ready (sometimes, indeed, almost uncomfortably so) to encourage innovation. Cardiff was accessible, and Raymond Garlick travelled there regularly for meetings of the Welsh Arts Council's first Literature Committee, on which he served from 1967 to 1972. Here he participated in the establishment of the system of support for publishers and writers in both languages which is now taken for granted. Llansteffan, too, was accessible: the family moved there in 1969, partly as a result of the enthusiastic advocacy of Tudor Bevan, with whom he shared an office; equally so was Gwasg Gomer at Llandysul which, between 1968 and 1976, published three handsome volumes, their covers bearing a representation of the Croix de Camargue

which stands near the gypsy pilgrimage church of Les Saintes Maries de la Mer, on the very edge of Europe, looking towards Africa.

The first, A SENSE OF EUROPE, COLLECTED POEMS 1954–1968, contained ten poems from THE WELSH-SPEAKING SEA, 'Blaenau Observed', and twenty-two

30

poems from LANDSCAPES AND FIGURES, but its largest section, 'A Sense of Europe', derives from the Dutch years.

The personal happiness of the early Trinity College years was marred only by Iestyn's serious illness (aplastic leukaemia), which held the family in agony from autumn 1968 to spring 1969:

> *we lived*
> *on that precipice,*
> *between the wall*
> *and the abyss;*
> *three of us trapped . . .*
> *('A Touch of White')*

The mortality rate from the disease was extremely high, but his recovery total.

What might be termed semi-official recognition of Raymond Garlick's view of Anglo-Welsh writing came in 1970 when the University of Wales Press published AN INTRODUCTION TO ANGLO-WELSH LITERATURE in its 'Writers of Wales' series. The term 'Anglo-Welsh' is attributed to Evan Evans (1731–88), the tradition traced back to 'Hymn to the Virgin' (*c.* 1470), probably by Ieuan ap Hywel Swrdwal (fl. 1430–80) – a work which Raymond Garlick would translate in 1985 when it was printed with his 'Introduction' in the beautiful Gwasg Gregynog edition. When Trinity College decided to establish a course in Welsh Studies in which Welsh and Anglo-Welsh literature were taught side by side, he was delighted to become Principal Lecturer in charge, a position he held until retirement. (His course was the first of its kind. Today similar courses are

common in Wales and the USA.) In 1972 also came A
SENSE OF TIME, POEMS AND ANTIPOEMS, of which an
unusual feature is overtly political poetry provoked
by the 1971 campaign by Cymdeithas yr Iaith during
which his wife, sister-in-law and son were arrested.
This was one way of living up to his *responsibility
towards the cultures and languages* of his adopted
country and his *duty to defend it.*

A meeting in 1973 with John Dressel of Webster
College, St Louis, led in 1976 to the establishment of
an American Programme linking Trinity College and
the Central University of Iowa. Raymond Garlick
contributed (and still does so today, in spite of his
retirement) an Anglo-Welsh component. The same
year saw the publication of INCENSE, POEMS
1972–1975, which completed a trilogy celebrating
Wales in Europe. Although a few poems deal with
civil rights, their tone is no longer strident.

By this time too, after more than twenty-five years,
the marriage was coming to an end. In 1977 came the
final separation and he moved with his daughter,
now a student, to live in a flat near Trinity College
(Elin settled in Amsterdam, to become a noted
translator of modern Dutch literature into Welsh).
And at about this time he deliberately put into
practice the principle enunciated by John Cowper
Powys in OBSTINATE CYMRIC *that the moment has
arrived for clearing my mind of cant.* Looking at his
own life, he came to the firm conclusion that he had
*never for one moment really thought that the
supernatural had existence,* and that all his life his
religious position *had not been belief but make-believe*
('A Small Boy in the Thirties', II, PLANET 103), though
with a warm affection for Catholicism as an

expression of European culture. A divorce, by mutual consent, ensued in 1982.

The extraordinary jingoism surrounding the Falklands adventure, in which the English establishment did not hesitate to involve Welsh soldiers yet again in colonialist conflict, produced (in his essay AUTHORS TAKE SIDES ON THE FALKLANDS, 1982) a characteristic reaction. After pointing out that

Since 1865 there has been a Welsh settlement in Patagonia . . . originating in oppression by British Conservative landlords in Wales at that time [and that] *the sending of the Welsh Guards to the Falklands . . . raised the possibility that Welshmen from Wales would be confronting Welshmen from Patagonia (as has indeed happened)*

he rejects all violence as barbarism, and concludes:

I am appalled at the sanctimoniousness and violence of British nationalism, the warmongering of most of the English tabloid newspapers, the attacks on free and reasoned speech and the BBC, the virtual collapse of democratic opposition in Parliament . . . The solution? Perpetual exile on the Falkland Islands for both Argentine and British juntas and their most strident supporters, there among the graves of their young victims to begin to learn together the elements of being adult, rational, civilized human beings.

In 1984 came the anthology, ANGLO-WELSH POETRY, 1480–1980, of which, (poetic justice!) he was responsible for the first, and Roland Mathias for the second half.

Shortly after the period of mature flowering, the poetic impulse failed:

33

I see from the last notebook in which I worked that 'Notes for an Autobiography' was completed on August 29th [1979]. Thereafter I wrote no more poems. I was in no doubt that the vein of poetry had run out, and accepted it.

('A Poet Looks Back', 1989)

So in 1987 he published COLLECTED POEMS, 1946–1986. It contains 121 poems, everything that the author wished to preserve from the seven volumes beginning with POEMS FROM THE MOUNTAIN-HOUSE (1950). Its appearance, a year after his retirement from full-time teaching,

discharged my last responsibility to an activity which no longer formed a part of my life. [It was time] *for a strategic withdrawal in order to concentrate all remaining energies upon the support of the life-force itself.*

At the end of the first week in March 1989, (the full story is told in 'A Poet Looks Back', LLAIS LLYFRAU) the impulse returned after a fine BBC programme on W. B. Yeats. By the end of the month, the most productive of his life, nine new poems had been written. The influence of the great Anglo-Irish poet upon the Anglo-Welsh has been so enormous that it is appropriate that he should have been the immediate stimulus for the fine new volume of 1992, TRAVEL NOTES. There was an influence from life also: to Garlick's unbounded delight, a grandchild, Alys, (Angharad's daughter) had been born in 1988, the year of his own voyage to Byzantium, a cruise around the eastern Mediterranean. As is characteristic of his best work, the collection unites humanity, literature and art.

In 1992, his autobiographical essay, 'Choosing Wales'

was included in Discovering Welshness (Gomer); 1993 and 1994 saw the paper '1944–1950: Dock Leaves and Nettles' read (13 March 1993) at the Gregynog Colloquium of the University of Wales Association for the Study of Welsh Writing in English (which owes its existence in great part to his work over many years), and a series of autobiographical pieces in Planet: 'A Small Boy in the Thirties', I, II and III (December 1993, February and April 1994), 'Portfolio' and 'Some Painters' (October and December 1994). 'Dylan Thomas and Others' and 'Mr Powys and Miss Playter' appeared in 1995. To all of these this essay owes a great debt.

II

Raymond Garlick's formation as a poet has been traced from the influence of good teaching to the timely challenge of Louis Soeterboek. As he has identified ('Inspiration and Perspiration') the influences which assisted his achievement of an individual voice, this is a good place to begin a detailed exploration of his verse.

What all the poems encountered from early childhood on had in common, [he writes] was a strong sense of structure. The precision with which English could be articulated, the grace of its sound, certainly led to a conscious determination to try to write and speak it as well as possible.

From Axel Munthe he acquired

a sense of style, a sense of Europe, a desire to travel and perhaps live abroad, a curiosity about Catholicism.

As a student he was fascinated by Plato's ION, in which Socrates

comes to the conclusion that a poet cannot compose anything worth calling poetry until he becomes inspired and as it were mad, and he talks about the degree in which the Muse itself has descended on him and put him in a state of divine insanity (Shelley's translation).

Raymond Garlick has not claimed this kind of inspiration for himself; he talks rather of *a predisposition to respond.*

He traces three influences which spoke to his particular condition and needs at a given moment: Dylan Thomas, Walter de la Mare and Roy Campbell. It was the technical skill to which he responded: originality of imagery (one thinks of 'Blaenplwyf', with its metaphor of the television mast as *goad but good*); precision of diction (characteristic of Raymond Garlick's own mature work); elegant structure ('Marwnad', the opening poem of A SENSE OF TIME is a good example of this), and *crystalline quality*. From Dylan Thomas he contrived to learn without those lapses into unintentionally humorous pastiche which afflicted his less discriminating admirers. From de la Mare's WINGED CHARIOT (1951) he learned how to use the rhymed triplet and quatrain and acquired the skill to handle long poems which 'Blaenau Observed' and 'Acclamation' demonstrate. He quotes as characteristic:

> Time sheened the splendour that was Absalom's hair;
> Time stilled the Garden; seduced Judas there;
> Sped the avenging blade for Robespierre;
> Dogged Marx, in reverie drowned, through Bloomsbury
>   Square.

Roy Campbell's poetry led him to the Camargue, where he found the emblem for his 1968–76 trilogy; he admired Campbell's rumbustious life and attacks on the literary establishment. A brief quotation from 'The Zebras' perhaps best illustrates what is meant by *crystalline quality*:

> The sunlight, zithering along their flanks with fire,
> Flashes between the shadows as they pass
> Barred with electric tremors through the grass
> Like wind along the golden strings of a lyre.

The Eerde years completed the process:

In the heart of Overijssel, one of the eastern and most rural Dutch provinces, the insulation of language and the Continental land-mass gave welcome relief from the Anglophone world and its obsessions, and a stimulating awareness of the closeness of new neighbours – Germany, Belgium, France. This certainly contributed to the sense of inner space and openness which enables emotion to be recollected in tranquillity and poems to be made.

A development initiated by a Dutchman from one part of the Netherlands had been completed by the atmosphere of another one. The equilibrium would be overset temporarily by the response of the authorities to the Welsh language campaign of the 1970s, much as Yeats's had been by the very much more violent (but by no means unconnected) events of Easter 1916. No *terrible beauty* was born, perhaps because, unpleasant as was the response of police and judiciary, there were, mercifully, no deaths.

POEMS MCMXLVII, stimulated by and shared with 'Louis Olav Leroi', was privately printed in 1947. Its successor, POEMS FROM THE MOUNTAIN-HOUSE, 1950, was published by Reginald Caton's Fortune Press, whose list included Philip Larkin (THE NORTH SHIP), Roy Fuller, Henry Treece, Glyn Jones and Dylan Thomas (18 POEMS). The first of its thirty-one short poems, 'Poem from the Mountain-House', evokes the strongly physical life of Llanllechid:

Life is the tautening of nerve and limb –
feet grappling with the mountain, thighs tense-sprung,
straddling lithe valleys, sheep and boulder slung,
splashing through rushes at lapping lake-brim.

– and a sense of its history as the domain of a loving God. 'Ghosts', the final poem, emphasizes the building's own long history of human occupation:

> Now memories like autumn leaves are blown
> through the still avenues of my mind;
> they are all gone, and I am here alone.

In this volume the influence of Gerard Manley Hopkins is strong: 'Eclogue' refers to *sky-dipped thrush eggs* and the *spurting* of a spring in which things are *birthed and feathered and fed*. 'Sonnet' echoes 'Glory be to God for Dappled Things' (*Praise to the all-good God for middle things*). In 'Storm' the influence of 'The Wreck of the Deutschland' is excessive:

> Cloud clash, thunder throb thickening, wind whine:
> lightning scythes sky, and stars are a-stagger
> and swamped; white-fire furrows . . .

Generally speaking, however, alliteration and echoing vowel-sounds give freshness and force:

> a jade green blade of grass darts from the hedge,
> turns lizard, and scurries across the path;
> blinks rapidly, whisks in its aftermath
> of tail, becoming grass at the other edge.

The poems divide almost equally into three sections. Those of the first are inspired by a natural scene, explicitly Welsh only in 'Aros a Myned', based on a poem of Ceiriog's translated by Elin. Even violent natural phenomena are viewed as aspects of God's mercy (Hopkins again), and harmony is suggested by such explicitly musical metaphors as *Grieg-music in the wind* and *a water symphony*. An engaging personality emerges in such colloquial touches as *There was no drama about it . . . yet it was very lovely just the same.* ('Eclogue') and *A very comfortable kind routine, / this life* ('Country Life').

The personality becomes whimsical in section II ('The Poet to his Cat', 'The Intellectual Snail', the latter poem reminding us of the enthusiasm for Lewis Carroll learned from his grandfather). This section, with its variety of work, including 'Ballet', 'Orchestra', 'Gandhi' and 'De Profundis', makes a transition from the God-suffused nature of I to the explicitly religious III. 'Vesper':

> *Lord of earth and sea and sky,*
> *you whom men did crucify . . .*

and 'A Christmas Carol':

> *Sleep on, my babe, in peace;*
> *the snow shall be a fleece*
> *to swathe and warm*
> *your tiny form*
> *until our winter cease.*

are hymns rather than lyrics and remind us of A. G. Prys-Jones. Both 'Exposition' and 'Orison' are specifically Roman Catholic and the dramatic lyric, 'Sermon from Padley' is attributed to a hypothetical ancestor,

The Venerable Nicholas Garlick, priest, one of the Padley Martyrs, [who] *suffered death at Derby on July 24th, 1588.*

The volume was noticed by Prys-Jones, who referred (typically) to

40

the courageous venture of a group of South Pembrokeshire writers who meet regularly to discuss their work and common interests

and went on to praise *a collection of high promise as well as of real achievement.* He noted the *influence and rhythms of Manley Hopkins* and summed up with:

his work is intense and vivid: it is completely intelligible without being formal or hackneyed. Abounding in verbal melody, colour and lyric beauty, it contains lovely, memorable lines. To his deep awareness of the natural and spiritual worlds, Mr Garlick adds a quiet humour.

In the WESTERN MAIL's 'Here and There' column appeared a response from Wil Ifan which tells us more about him than it does about Raymond Garlick, but quotes with approval from 'Country Life' and 'Orchestra' and describes *this new poet* as one who *had used his eyes to some purpose.* Dilys Rowe, oddly, found the work *facile.*

The tragically early death of the promising Welsh poet, R. Aled Hughes, produced REQUIEM FOR A POET, the most specifically Catholic of Raymond Garlick's works. This commissioned *radio ode,* broadcast from Cardiff by the BBC and from Dublin by Radio Eiréann, was published as a DOCK LEAVES pamphlet in 1954. 'Wales Day by Day' in the WESTERN MAIL commented: [it] *breaks new ground in Wales as regards its form* [by following] *the pattern of the liturgy for the departed.* Prys-Jones found it *impressive.*

By the time THE WELSH-SPEAKING SEA was published by the Dock Leaves Press in 1954, Raymond Garlick had been editor of DOCK LEAVES for five years. He

41

was beginning to move on equal terms with Welsh- and English-medium writers. In editorials, the DUBLIN MAGAZINE and the WELSH ANVIL, he was developing his theory of Anglo-Welsh writing. He had become a father (the collection is dedicated jointly to Elin and Iestyn) and was becoming an experienced teacher. The volume begins with two confident claims on his adopted country: its epigraph, from John Davies of Hereford:

> *If my words be unfit,*
> *That blame be mine; but if Wales better be*
> *By my disgrace; I hold that grace to me.*

and its first lyric, 'Poem for my Son':

> *To you I give a golden garden, Wales,*
> *to play in: half a hundred voels and vales*
> *shall be your toys, and you shall sing and laugh*
> *amid a noise of flights of nightingales.*

Superficially the style is that of POEMS FROM THE MOUNTAIN-HOUSE – rhyme, regular metre, alliteration, vowel-music – but improved, sure of itself and its subject matter. Only one poem from the first volume's thirty-one ('Orchestra', re-titled 'Barbirolli') would appear in the rigorous COLLECTED POEMS of 1987 compared to four from this volume's twenty-nine. What is more, these are characteristic of the mature poet: 'Biographical Note', 'Dylan Thomas at Tenby' (re-titled), 'Tenby' and 'Dyfed'.

Like those of POEMS FROM THE MOUNTAIN-HOUSE, the contents are organized into three sections: 'The Land', 'People' and 'The Word', though more than half are in the first section. Like Prys-Jones, of whom there are further echoes ('Here on the Furthest Western Edge of Wales' being the strongest), Raymond Garlick celebrates a beautiful *rural* Wales, steeped in history and legend:

Dyfed where Pryderi used to ride
. . . where beside,
his bay Giraldus watched the lawn-sleeved tide . . .

('Dyfed')

Gerallt grandson of Nest . . .
Dylan son of Aranrhod, young sea-god . . .

('Poem from Manorbier')

the silver knights
of Stackpole Elidore

('Barafundle')

the pirate island with the cruel Norse name . . .

('Journey to Skomer')

Essentially this landscape is South Pembrokeshire and, as the volume's title promises, the sea is powerfully present (speaking elegant English). Sea imagery and sea rhythms abound:

wind-frilled water heaves; the break of waves and the rake
of surf

('Poem from Manorbier')

the spinning waters rise and seem to weave
a silk that rides the breakers when they fall,
a taut, transparent skin . . .

('Ebb Tide')

waving weeds and weaving water-lights

('Barafundle')

The delight of a young poet sure of his subject is evident not only in rhythm, verbal music and rhyme, but in imagery both apt and witty:

oysters
share the prayer of prawns in moist profundity
('Poem from Manorbier')

waves . . . with prim and poodle leaps
('Tenby')

A boast of boys and a giggle of girls
('Journey to Skomer')

Details of the natural scene are fixed in precise, sometimes almost heraldic imagery:

slanted slab-cake cliffs in tiers of pink
and praline browse and tilt
('Barafundle')

silken sand –
saffron and smooth
('Journey to Skomer')

A lighthouse put a finger forth to gild
black seas
('The Elate Island')

'The Poet Reads his Play at Tenby' ('Dylan Thomas at Tenby' in later volumes), celebrating the performance of October 1953, is the most memorable poem in the 'People' section, and the best in the volume. It exemplifies Raymond Garlick's ability to balance high seriousness with a wit that often has the mischief of whimsy. The atmosphere of the provincial occasion is beautifully caught: *Into the pause while peppermints were passed*, and the poet neatly characterized:

expressionless of face: politely bored; lit a cigarette,
screwing his eyes up in the smart of smoke.

The excitement of the reading is enhanced by contrast:

> *Now the sleeping town. . .*

> *. . . strode heron-stilted through the dark*
> *and rode white horses, nightmares from the sea,*
> *across a cantref of this bay's bright arc . . .*

and the drama completed by restrained allusion:

> *It was October, the month of birthdays.*
> *The saga was nearly ended.*

A brief elegy, 'Poem for Dylan', appears in the volume's third section, 'The Word':

> *Now there is laughter in heaven: but after,*
> *winter limps into the silent, empty west.*

and his influence, assimilated, may be found in such lines as:

> *There is a candle lanterned in the ribs*
> *no hand has held, no bell has called, no man*
> *has lit.*
>
> ('The Candle')

where it combines (as in the early poetry of T. H. Jones) with that of Yeats:

> *At midnight on the Emperor's pavement flit*
> *Flames that no faggot feeds, nor steel has lit,*
> *Nor storm disturbs, flames begotten of flame . . .*
>
> ('Byzantium')

The 'People' section contains the delightful portrait of a schoolboy, Jones:

> *Apple-cheeked ink-dappled wriggling jack*
> *boxed in a niggling desk . . .*

and, with 'Parisians', carries the volume into Europe.

'The Word' section is about learning to speak (in 'Poem' the child's consonants imitate those of the sea in which he paddles), teaching ('Lower VI Arts' – *a rope / of reason tying them to my tongue*), writing poetry, and the Word of God. Its finest poem, shorn of its first triplet:

> *My dimensions are Wales and twenty-seven*
> *years. I am eight wounds of my way to death:*
> *they have nine lives whom the muse has shriven.*

has survived into the COLLECTED POEMS. With characteristic self-pitiless candour, it evokes his disability:

> *I live in a rakish body framed*
> *about a spine like a buckled spire . . .*

(an extraordinary image) and contrasting, compensatory artistic ability:

> *to poise and pin*
>
> *a pattern on deformity, to voice*
> *the un-neat not known . . .*

The intentional clumsiness of *un-neat not known* is extremely effective. The penultimate line, *a hustings of a heart wrapped in a rack*, clinches the self-characterization with characteristic wit.

The volume shows significant development. Prys-

Jones, reviewing it under the headline *Lyric Poet* in the Western Mail (24 April 1955) understandably approved of poems which, like his own, *breathe the high romance of by-gone days*. He described 'The Poet Reads his Play at Tenby' as *an admirable piece of work* and summed up:

Mr Garlick is a meticulous craftsman who uses alliteration and assonance to fine effect . . . as a whole these poems reveal a passionate love of Wales, its language and traditions. They are appealing and melodious, simple and sincere . . .

On 10 October 1955 The Welsh-Speaking Sea was one of the four entries to reach the final round for the John Llewelyn Rhys Prize, presented at the National Book League that year by Emlyn Williams. Helen Rhys wrote:

It is, I think, only the second time that a book of poems has been among the finalists since the prize was founded, in 1940.

The 1957 volume Blaenau Observed is dedicated to *my Neighbour and Friend John Cowper Powys* and *the Chorus* (the people of the town). Sections of it had appeared in Y Ddinas, the Dublin Magazine and the New York Times Book Review before its broadcast on the Welsh Home Service on 14 June 1956 and subsequent publication as a Dock Leaves pamphlet. It has a powerful epigraph from Rilke:

That we are in circumstances which work upon us, which set us free from time to time to face things that are great and natural, is all that is necessary.

Any poetic evocation of a small Welsh town is likely to be indebted to Under Milk Wood, but this one owes little more than the basic idea. Its form is rhymed triplets and its metre is best described as iambic pentameter relaxed in the direction of contemporary speech-rhythm. The opening line, for example – *It is morning, early morning in May* – although possessing ten syllables, is pure colloquial; a line like *Frontstage, a crowd of buildings – blue and grey*, is regular iambic after the initial trochee. This is well calculated for radio performance. The seven scenes evoke the life, setting and history of the town from an early morning in May to an evening in the same month, with a flashback, in scene four, to winter.

Scene one presents the town as a stage upon which the poem's drama will be presented:

> *Swaying slightly, the mist has shuddered up*
> *shewing a soft-lit, silent, empty set*
> *– an amphitheatre mounted in a cup*
>
> *of mountains. Horseshoe-shaped, the stage stands high*
> *on a rock-rigged platform. Beneath it curves*
> *the valley floor. The backcloth is the sky,*
>
> *and, piercing this, pure pyramids of slate*
> *heaped neatly on the hills; a peak or two;*
> *some kind of quarry mast that rises straight*
>
> *and silver from the centre of the scene.*
> *Frontstage, a crowd of buildings – blue and grey –*
> *smoke into life. The wings are washed in green.*

The content is as far from *the high romance of by-gone days* as the style from the neat quatrain and sonnet so common in the first two collections. The conceit disappears under the precise detail of plain diction; sentences are skilfully carried over the three-line form; it is a delight to read aloud. This is the work of a poet who has found his voice and uses it with confidence.

In section two, from the County School set on the valley's edge, the schoolteacher/poet looks out on a wider scene:

> past the low-walled ledge
>
> of school yard, past the palisade of pines,
> down to the canyon of Cwm Bowydd deep
> below – a trough of mist fluffing the lines
>
> of river and wood.

In the five minutes before teaching begins, he thinks of the part played by Wales in the history of Europe, introducing it with an echo of THE WASTE LAND:

> And sometimes in its turning I can hear
> the ring of feet upon a street in Troy
> and Helen singing as she braids her hair,
>
> or Socrates in some suburban shop . . .
>
> Soon, far from home in some brash Oxford tower,
> Ieuan ap Hywel Swrdwal maps a rhyme . . .
>
> In the city of Deiniol Shakespeare invests
> the Archdeacon's house with Glendower's voice . . .

and he contrasts Welsh rural life:

> knocker and door-knob kneaded, steps blenched clean,
> new polished parlour, candlesticks aglint,
> and Salem on the wall . . .

with that of Swansea and Cardiff.

It is easier for a Roman Catholic than for an Anglican or Nonconformist to manage this kind of perspective – indeed, his religion enforces it. Scene three presents *The papist church beside the school* with its *golden feast . . . rainbow-raking joy in heaven and earth*. He remembers being distracted from Mass one Sunday by a squirrel in a nearby tree and wondering *how Dafydd ap Gwilym might handle this*. Section four, evoking winter in imagery reminiscent of THE WELSH-SPEAKING SEA:

> *the peaks are topped with cones of strawberry ice,*
> *the hills slide into solid marble slabs . . .*

carries the perspective into the life of cities, which *in the tasting, charm; / drunk daily to the dregs they stun the sense*, evoking his own experience of Spezia, Rouen, Bangor, Madrid, before returning to Blaenau in winter to meditate on human perception:

> *What then is dream, and what reality?*
> *All* seems; *what* is? *Or is the womb of truth*
> *imagination's white immensity?*
>
> *Do your eyes see what mine see?*

After presenting the *ancient landscape* of Wales from the perspective of a Rome seen as forming it and nursing it to nationhood, and wondering, as he returns from school in the late afternoon, how his son, his *small face posted at the window pane*, with his *small boy's sight – bright as a bird's and candid as the moon* is viewing the scene, he introduces the

> *Chorus, hidden and unseen*
> *in private Green Rooms – kitchens, parlours, bars*

and his friend, Mr Powys:

> *And you, my neighbour and friend, whose tireless pen*
> *has pinned to paper mysteries unseen*

viewed with awe and curiosity by the locals:

> *Thus, darkly infidel, and yet most proud,*
> *heads are upturned towards the window square*
> *that frames you writing, reading. Watch that crowd*
> *of cheeping children down below at play:*
> *see them look up, waiting the fluttered hand*
> *before they turn again and run away.*

It is with the perspective of this distinguished Anglo-Welsh writer, descended perhaps from a Welsh lord of the seventeenth century, with Donne and Cowper among his maternal ancestors, that the poem appropriately closes:

> *You make us pause; survey ourselves again*
> *– catching a glimpse not merely of a town*
> *notorious as the native place of rain,*
>
> *but of a stage for human history*
> *superb as the theatre of Perikles.*
> *Poised amid peaks, we find our dignity.*

As the epigraph promised, *things that are great and natural* have been faced. Both technically and in its human and artistic range, the poem marks further advances. Here is the characteristic mature work of this poet: at the centre, Wales, its history, landscape, people, art, but a Wales which has contributed and continues to contribute to the civilization of Europe. The perception, though deeply serious, is balanced by affectionate humour.

Raymond Garlick handed over the editorial chair of the ANGLO-WELSH REVIEW to Roland Mathias when he moved to Eerde in 1960. Ten years after THE WELSH-SPEAKING SEA and seven after BLAENAU OBSERVED, he could find only twenty-seven poems for LANDSCAPES AND FIGURES, published, in a limited edition, by the Merrythought Press in 1964. It is subtitled, and rightly so, SELECTED POEMS 1949–1963, for 'Orchestra' and 'Ballet' (re-titled 'Barbirolli' and 'Ballerina') are reprinted from POEMS FROM THE MOUNTAIN-HOUSE and 'Expedition Skomer' and 'Biographical Note' (without its opening stanza) from THE WELSH-SPEAKING SEA. The volume is dedicated *for Eerde with thanks*.

There are interesting developments in form and subject-matter: a dozen or so poems are written in short-lined (mostly two-, occasionally three-stressed) quatrains and three are what the author calls

shaped poems . . . derived from [Dylan Thomas's] *'Vision and Prayer', from Rhydwen Williams in 'Cerddi Cadwgan', and from the probable Anglo-Welsh source of it all, George Herbert.*
('Inspiration and Perspiration')

The most interesting example is the powerful opening poem, 'Vowels', of which the first stanza exemplifies both form and content:

A
is life,
a sharp grass ray
green as the apple that Adam's wife
plucked from the spray
that leaf-rife
day.

This poem is literally about *the colour of saying*, for Raymond Garlick sees not merely vowels, but entire words, in colour:

The perceived word is read in unperceived colour, transfused through the word by its vowels – A apple-green, E gold, I ink-black; O is ivory, and U the blue of the umbrellas in Renoir's Parapluies *in the London National Gallery . . . How satisfying that* grass *should have a green vowel, and* ink *a black one, that so many of the words of religion enclose whiteness. What a halcyon word is* plenitude, *for example, the gold and blue wings of its first and last syllables balanced upon the ebony vertical at its centre.* (Artists in Wales, 2)

Synaesthesia is not uncommon among artists – Rimbaud's 'Voyelles', for example, opens with:

A noir, E blanc, I rouge, O bleu: voyelles,
Je dirai quelque jour vos naissances latentes . . .

and the novelist/poet, Vladimir Nabokov, has written about it. An early example in Raymond Garlick's work is the evocation in 'Orchestra' of music in terms of architecture:

he cries for a crescendo and they bound
and fly like buttresses to the tall spire
of his baton . . .

No doubt his life's linked preoccupations with words, visual art and music are related to this.

The combination of form and style in 'Vowels' is particularly happy. 'The Cardigan Pilgrimage', a specifically Catholic lyric, and 'Reading the Adonais' are similarly structured. Shaped poems, never common, die away after A SENSE OF TIME and poems in the short-lined quatrains after INCENSE.

Although working in the Netherlands, he continued to spend part of each year in Wales. By including in LANDSCAPES AND FIGURES two poems from each of his previous collections, he presumably wished to emphasize continuity. 'Biographical Note' is complemented by 'Indirect Speech':

> *Trapped in a sack of bones swinging askew*
> *which no imperative of flesh can snap*
> *back into symmetry, the neat sinew*
>
> *of speech alone is sane.*

and the two MOUNTAIN-HOUSE poems by 'Picasso's Femme Qui Pleure'. The portrait of a tyrannical teacher in 'Prize Day':

> *The watered silks*
> *do not disguise*
> *corrosive voice*
> *and acid eyes:*
>
> *he is a hater.*

and the poem 'The Immortals' recalls experiences at Blaenau. The majority of the volume derives from Welsh, not Dutch experience, 'Against Plato's Theory of Forms' and 'Astigmatism' developing ideas about the nature of perception raised in BLAENAU OBSERVED. Wales is seen with greater detachment, though no less affection. 'Wenvoe and Blaen-Plwyf' and 'Seeing' advance a point of view interestingly different from that of his friend, R. S.

Thomas – television as an influence for unity in a Wales that was once *a mere abstraction,* a place where

> Only the highest tide of news would lap
> over the Moelwyn peaks.

It seems reasonable to suppose, since this is the form chosen for poems about the Netherlands, that the short-lined quatrain is connected with that country's neat orderliness. Seven such poems constitute the heart of the volume. 'Note on the Iliad' evokes with relish the emergence of new land:

> the polder surfaced
> sleek as a whale
> and still awash.
> Then the last veil
>
> of standing water
> slides away.

and the closing moral:

> Hard . . .
> to imagine this:
> a people at grips
> with genesis
> not apocalypse.

circles back to the opening question:

> Why are epics
> always about
> the anti-life
> of a noble lout?

There is a sense of a landscape refreshingly wider –

immense
diagonals light
the gothic forest; deer
through the antlered woods.

'Still Life' portrays a wild boar, *a ton of brush,* as *the forest itself* approaching consciousness. The poet and his family, at home, adjusted, are seen in 'Note on the Iliad' enjoying their picnic on what used to be the North Sea's floor; in 'Collector's Piece' the two children return from a country walk with their trophies – *silky feathers, a basket of berries*:

Side by side
silent, treading the chrome
and crimson forest
they harvest home.

Within a year of the return to Wales, stimulated by the new challenge of college teaching (he has told me that the requirement to meet a deadline, in the assessment of assignments, for example, always, with paradoxical inconvenience, inspired poems) Raymond Garlick produced a much more extensive response to European experience, his COLLECTED POEMS 1954–1968, under the title A SENSE OF EUROPE. The volume is dedicated to Iestyn and Angharad, the children of 'Collector's Piece'. Continuity is firmly established by the retention of ten poems from THE WELSH-SPEAKING SEA, BLAENAU OBSERVED and all of LANDSCAPE AND FIGURES except the unique oddity, 'Mexican in Wales', and two poems from MOUNTAIN-HOUSE. There are thirty-eight new poems, almost every one of which could be said to reflect the volume's title.

'Baling Out', the first of the new poems, develops the

theme of 'Biographical Note' and 'Indirect Speech':

> *Be my escape, my parachute,*
> *fabric of words; unshut for me*
> *your cupola to catch my shout*
> *and calm it to a silver curve.*

Experience of Europe, development of the Anglo-Welsh theme and growing militancy in support of the Welsh language campaign lead to further exploration of the poet's craft and role. 'After Lévi-Strauss' characteristically brings together Cricieth, Solutré and the Netherlands to forge an image of the kind of poetry that is required now:

> *incisive and hard.*
> *This Solutrean blade*
> *is a kind of poem*
> *a man once made*
>
> *a new precision*
> *pared out of flint,*
> *its message poised*
> *in the craft's glint.*

'Consider Kyffin' calls in aid the whole Anglo-Welsh tradition (it must never be forgotten that this poet is a teacher):

> *In silted bays of old bookshops –*
> *shelved and becalmed like ancient ships*
> *in saffron havens, I have rocked*
> *their boats, long run aground and wrecked;*
> *eased dusty covers open, looked,*
> *clambered inside entranced, unlocked*
> *each bulkhead page from stern to beak*
> *and in the cabin of his book*
> *come on the poet at his ease.*

to castigate Welsh ignorance of heritage:

> *They are the root from which you stem –*
> *but you have never heard of them.*

'Personal Statement' moves from a definition of craft:

> *for me a poem is first a frame.*
> *Form is the cane on which I lean.*

to one of purpose:

> *These syllables swarm*
> *in Wales, Europe. Europe and Wales*
> *commit them to a theme and form.*

'Point of Departure' rounds the volume off with a re-statement of the Solutré image – words honed by long tradition:

> *Dart,*
> *then, words – shining sharp*
> *and obsidian. Art*
> *must fit and flight from its bow-taut harp*
> *precisions of the clumsy heart.*

In earlier volumes it is easy to pick out individual themes, and the poet helps us by grouping the poetry in sections (*Land, People, Word* for example). It is more difficult here, although a simple lyric such as 'Wales' or the beautiful, acerbic 'Notes for a Picture':

> *Gothic Eryri's*
> *aquatint*
> *and Wyddfa clear-lined*
> *as a print*

> *hang on the sky,*
> *remote as art,*
> *while tourists tear*
> *their names apart.*

are easy to classify, as is 'In the National Museum'. Similarly, there are poems *simply* about the Netherlands ('Kruupweg', 'Ommen Forest') or other parts of Europe ('Camargue', 'Camargue Cross'). Maturity, however, brings complexity; perspective, integration. 'After Donne' exemplifies its title only to the extent of employing the well-known quotation, *no man is an island*, to define Europeanism:

> *The lane round which*
> *your village sprawls*
> *can wind you under*
> *the Kremlin walls . . .*

'Academic Overture' uses an archetypal image – the Chancellor of the Belgian University of Louvain walking unperturbed through a violent demonstration – to caution Welsh people against extremism:

> *and when the roar*
>
> *of fanatic slogans*
> *beats in your brain,*
> *remember the Chancellor*
> *of Louvain.*

'Matters Arising' similarly combines the resonant events of Easter 1916 in Ireland (*In Wales we shall never see / a terrible beauty born*) and the tolerance of the Netherlands to offer a paradigm for the Welsh patriot:

a freedom hacked out here
is a freedom without worth,
a terror without beauty.
Here it must come to birth . . .
as . . .
. . . the dove that broods on chaos –
wise as a thousand springs.

The Netherlands were invaded by Nazi Germany in early May 1940, and it was not until May 1945, that the Nazis were expelled. On 5 May the Dutch celebrate their liberation, but on the previous day, Herdenkingsdag (Remembrance Day), they honour those who suffered, in particular the Jews. Although Eerde was a most beautiful and peaceful setting, the Quaker school for Jewish children which had existed in the castle during the period of occupation suffered bitterly: in 1943, its pupils and their teacher were taken away to a Polish concentration camp and never heard of again. In May 1966, Raymond Garlick wrote 'Fourth of May', a poem which provoked sufficient discussion and correspondence later, in the ANGLO-WELSH REVIEW, for him to explain it at some length:

in 1965 or early 1966 I saw two . . . film reports which were very disturbing. The first was about para-military activities in Ulster . . . the second . . . about the Free Wales Army. A number of men, booted, wearing para-military equipment, and apparently carrying weapons, were filmed and interviewed – against a pastoral background of fields and forest not a little reminiscent of Eerde – as they engaged in a seemingly amateurish manner in various military activities. A lifelong pacifist, I was appalled.

The poem evokes Nazi violence abroad – *women and*

children / crucified here – to warn against extremism at home:

> *I think of this*
> *and remember Wales,*
> *the size of Holland.*
> *Don't let the nails*
>
> *of crucifixion*
> *be hammered there –*
> *employed by hands*
> *half unaware.*

Raymond Garlick comments:

I could only hope that in pastoral Wales – for centuries untouched by bloodshed, unaware of planned violence as a local, rural experience – such things would never happen. Like a number of others written at Eerde, 'Fourth of May' is an explicitly anti-violent peace poem . . . The Caernarfon event [the Investiture of the Prince of Wales] was indirectly the occasion of the self-destruction of two men and the maiming of a young boy. To my grief, 'Fourth of May' was less misjudged than I had imagined.

'At Camelot' and 'Monsignor Tudor' exemplify the poet's *sense of Europe*. The first traces the legends of Arthur, Gawain and Guinevere to Modena and beyond. By them Europe was made *golden . . . / from Wales to Spain*. Monsignor Tudor, in the eponymous dramatic monologue, exiled from:

> *the life that might have been*
> *(a Cardiff curacy, the year on year*
> *of priesthood in remote Caernarvonshire:*
> *to be the means of grace to one's own nation)*

feels guilty, seeks an excuse in God's will, but cannot help hearing *a persistent undertone*. Raymond Garlick, comfortable at Eerde and toying with the idea of Dutch citizenship, heard something similar – and returned home to attempt, as teacher and poet, to be *a means of grace* to his chosen nation.

A SENSE OF TIME is the most resonant of Raymond Garlick's titles. Time features as prehistory – the *pale / blue interstrata poised / among the purple* of the Old Red Sandstone measures on Llansteffan beach; personal history – University College, Bangor, in 1944; Welsh, European and world history. There is a sense of time mis-spent, lessons of history unlearned: Waterloo fought for the benefit of the Belgian tourist industry, 600 years of Welsh history *with nothing learned, / nothing forgotten*. The poet's exasperation gives this volume a satirical edge not felt before, and the centre of it is Wales. We can be more specific: 'Documentary', 'Anthem for Doomed Youth' and 'Passion 72' give us contemporary times, places and occasions to set against those of the past: 8 May 1971; 22 Tachwedd 1971, Swansea; 9 Chwefror 1972, Mold and Swansea. 'Aneirin Speaks' emphasizes personal involvement:

> *So I*
> *with wife, with sister-in-law, son, all*
> *arrested within eight days*
> *for the cause of the language.*

'Inspiration and Perspiration' explains how:

Shortly after the permanent return to Wales in 1967, life pulled out another drawer and scattered a whole series of new pictures which, very unexpectedly, were to give rise to a lot of new

poems: a police boot on a hand, young people dragged by the
hair, court scenes reminiscent of Daumier, respectable citizens
standing in the dock, the gates of Swansea and Cardiff prisons.
This was a context, these were scenes, for which one was almost
totally unprepared (apart from detached observation of
something not dissimilar in Flanders), but they were at once felt
to fit into the general pattern of growing Civil Rights awareness
of the time, where colour or religion were the issues elsewhere,
and language here. Most poetry originates in the emotions of
wonder, love, grief, but these events gave rise to an emotion
which Gwenallt in Welsh and Idris Davies in English had
shown could be productive of poetry, namely anger.

Eleven of the collection's fifty-one poems, grouped
more or less at its centre, deal with the language
campaign and the authorities' heavy-handed
reaction to it. 'Documentary', a concrete poem,
opens the sequence by picturing, most literally in
section 4:

> *Along*   *each side*
> *two files*   *in black*
> *advance.*

– a sit-down protest outside the Brangwyn Hall.
Section 1 pictures the crowd as a *lake, a pool of quiet in*
the sun and this image is effectively continued
through the poem – *shores / surface / flows in / pours*
into streams and strengthened in section 3 by the
further comparison, to a field of wheat into which
policemen *try to cut their swathe.* The crowd, of
young people, their parents, professors, ministers,
united in song, will not be provoked by the violence
of the police and is, in the outcome, triumphant:

> *The prisoners will be released at once,*
> *two of them without charges. Yet for this*

> *the police have put the public at risk,*
> *trampled on women, on their own image,*
> *arrested forty citizens for sitting still,*
> *discredited the law . . .*

'Anthem for Doomed Youth' (the allusion to Wilfred Owen's bitter protest about the meaningless slaughter of young men in the First World War is disproportionate) pays tribute to three young people brought to trial at Swansea, using a similar contrast – *soft chrysanthemum light* and *the radiance of the uncorrupted rose* against *bitter city* and *crucified*. 'Passion 72' tries to put unjust justice into perspective by invoking Socrates, Christ and Portia, Pilate, Moscow and Ulster, and concludes with the implausible suggestion that *the police, the scribe / and the pharisee* will be conscience-troubled in old age.

Judges are satirized: *rabbit fur / royal fig* ('The Judge's Tale'), *bogus hair and hunting pink / Staffordshire dogs* ('Judgement Day') and, in schoolmasterly tones, patronized in 'Public Gallery':

> *I sit and observe you over my glasses.*
> *Conduct like this would not do in my classes.*

In 'Ghosts' they become:

> *eyes that stare down from the bench*
> *not at citizens but pigs,*
> *baboons fantasy has bred*

– lines that contrast uncomfortably with the convincing dignity of the young man in 'Documentary' who *sternly forbids the shouting of abuse* and *restarts the singing.*

It is true that Gwenallt in Welsh and Idris Davies in English (we may add Jonathan Swift, Wilfred Owen and W. B. Yeats) made art out of anger. It is incontestable that Raymond Garlick's anger is justified. It produces its most effective poetry where, as in 'Lunch Break', it is contained by historical/ cultural perspective and embodied in appropriate imagery. Set

> *at Aust, where the Bridge springs*
> *to its feet by the spinnings*
> *of the Severn*

this poem opens with the rejection of *Austin bishop /* *of Canterbury* by the Welsh prelates who *withdrew /* *across the water to Wales / and civilisation*. This symbol allows it to conclude, without stridency:

> *You ask at*
> *whom I raise my fingertip?*
> *Instances, you ask? Just dip*
> *your hand and see which you pull*
> *out. Judges, for example.*

It is true also that, as Yeats pointed out, poets make poetry out of their quarrel with themselves, out of their quarrels with others, rhetoric. Raymond Garlick's angriest reactions to injustice are rhetoric at best. Too often they fall into bathos:

> *Vans begin to*
> *arrive, one or*
> *two containing*
> *dogs, though these were*
> *in fact not used.*

('Documentary')

portentousness:

> *With the cameras of language*
> *the antipoem must be shot,*
> *the precise documentary*
> *of the inexorable word.*
>
> ('Documentary')

even something close to hysteria:

> *what fate*
>
> *have the history books in store for you,*
> *while conscience is crucified in court?*
> ('Anthem for Doomed Youth')

The decorum usually so characteristic of this fine poet is lost: heart baffles head. Although Raymond Garlick has (rightly) reprinted a number of the protest-poems in the COLLECTED POEMS of 1987, I believe he is aware of this, for the quotation with which I began (p.63) continues: *The main form of writing to which it gave rise was in fact the letter.* I have no doubt that the angry correspondence was courteous, decorous, and extremely effective.

Raymond Garlick is, after all, too good a teacher not to know that it is a waste of time shouting, even at naughty boys. He has an endearing sense of humour and an acerbic wit, both of them active in his prose and elsewhere in this volume. 'Snapshot' gives an effective portrait of a tyrant – *This half-English Prussian . . . that coal-bucket on his head . . . The double-bed sized mantle* – and a very funny summing-up of the idle, unscrupulous rich:

> *It's curious how real*
> *estate accompanies reckless*

> *malefactors of this class*
> *into exile: mere train robbers*
> *seem naive as the three bears.*
> *Not to be parted from their porridge*
> *is an old royal privilege.*

Words like *real, malefactors, mere* and *porridge* (even if it does miss the pun) are brilliantly chosen and placed. The portrait of dowdy Dutch royalty in 'Oranges and Lemons' also reminds us of the childhood experiences of royalty and privilege in London.

The most effective poem of protest in this volume is 'Involvement'. With a combination of pathos (*an old man weeps . . . my numbed hand wipes / his streaming tears*) and scorn (*Cakes and circuses – / profits of tours, / and a pantomime / in Caernarfon towers*) it links the trials of one small European country with the rape of another and concludes:

> *In Wenceslas Square*
> *an old man's eyes*
> *melt for his fatherland*
> *and us.*

(The use of assonantal rhyme here is an apt allusion to Wilfred Owen.)

Raymond Garlick's finest contribution to the cause of the language is 'Bilingualism', a perfect and characteristic lyric and a poem which every child of school age in Wales ought to be encouraged to have by heart:

> *Athwart the canal, green as Wales,*
> *the great barge drifts. The tow-rope trails*

slack in the water. On the bank
the barge-horse grazes, polished flank
turned to the water. Huge as an ark
the barge slides on: its tarred planks bark
the further shore, pointing away
to nowhere in the hot midday.
Browsing on, the indifferent horse
leaves the ark to its calm non-course
as time laps by.

The problem's how
to turn the horse and the barge's prow
in one direction, harness each
to the other one before this reach
stills to a pool of green pondweeds
and, nose to stern across the reeds,
the barge lies like a monolith,
the stabled horse dies into myth,
means of communication silt
into a water-garden spilt
with dragon-flies, and marsh-worts sway
for picnickers on holiday.

Our immediate impression is of emblematic simplicity – a summer day in remote countryside, the still canal, the massive barge, the contrasting, powerful horse. The distinctive movement, the sense eddying gently across line endings, emphasizes the still point. Specific detail is painted in with simple, vivid language – *green/great/trails/slack/polished* – and the effect of this is enhanced by discreet alliteration (also operating across lines): *green/great/barge, tow-rope/trails/water*. The vowel music of the rhymes (so many of them on long *a* and *o* sounds) is extended by assonances and echoes: *Wales/great/grazes, leaves/calm/laps*, and the still music of the first stanza is further enhanced by the jarring contrast of *tarred planks bark*.

After the first stanza's statement of the problem –
picturesque stalemate, we might call it – the second
opens with quiet energy as the problem is addressed
– *The problem's how / to turn the horse . . .* – before
returning, in its final lines, to stagnation. The effect
of a first reading is of a simple, striking picture
powerfully conveyed by a brilliantly deployed range
of poetic effects.

With the picture memorably established, the
symbolism comes into effect. That the setting is rural
and the season summer is appropriate both to the
parts of Wales which are most bilingual and to the
suggestion, common in Raymond Garlick's poetry as
in that of R. S. Thomas, that rural (we may now add
once-industrial) Wales is in danger of becoming little
more than a playground for tourists. For a variety of
reasons, the choice of a canal as the channel of
communication is extremely appropriate, implying,
for example, history and tradition, a gentler way of
life. The horse, archetypal image, especially in Celtic
writing, contrasts with its burden (*polished
flank/tarred planks*) – the point once more underlined
by verbal echo – and when both are taken up again
in the second stanza, the barge becoming a *monolith*
and the horse a *myth*, we think of other monuments
to lost civilization. Even the apparently innocent
water-garden spilt / with dragon-*flies* is, in this context,
resonant.

Everything that is best in Raymond Garlick's art
unites in this long-meditated lyric. This is how a *poet*
serves his country – branding an archetype into the
mind, enacting, for those who have thought little or
nothing of it, the essence of a human problem. It is
not unreasonable to compare the central image of

this poem with that of Yeats's anguished 'Easter 1916':

> *Hearts with one purpose alone*
> *Through summer and winter seem*
> *Enchanted to a stone*
> *To trouble the living stream . . .*

where the fulness and changing beauty of life are contrasted with the mean-mindedness of obsession. We may also remind ourselves of Auden's lines ('In Memory of W. B. Yeats'):

> *poetry makes nothing happen: it survives*
> *In the valley of its saying . . .*
> *A way of happening, a mouth.*

– its function to *Teach the free man how to praise.*

There are other fine poems in this volume. 'Marwnad', for example, the plangent *shaped poem* in memory of the Pembrokeshire-born Waldo Williams, who died in 1971:

> *For*
> *Waldo*
> *open the door*
> *of silence. Let words blow*
> *down the world's winds. Let language soar*
> *for him, and swift verbs flow*
> *who on their shore*
> *chants no*
> *more.*

and 'Acclamation', commissioned by the Arts Council and broadcast on Radio Wales on 24

February 1972; but my favourites are those inspired by life at Llansteffan.

'Cywydd i Lansteffan' pictures

> the long ostrich fans
> of the plumed sea winnowing
> the two bays, the peacock wing
> of the tide folded towards
> the sunset

before focusing on the poet's emblematic home:

> Among trees,
> menhirs, fox-coloured bracken
> dense over barrow and den
> and set, our badger-lustrous
> black and white, committed house.

'Traeth Llansteffan' is a fine picture in sound (*the insistent sigh / of the respiring / sea*) and colour:

> The scoured rocks dry,
> sculptured and matt, ice-blue
> and Tyrian, acid as inks.

'Agincourt', another deceptively simple historical emblem, presents, in a way typical of this volume, the seven Welsh archers from the village who fought in *the bonemeal verdant meadows* where

> blood
> clotted the buttercups' sheen
> and the earth was disembowelled

and concludes:

And far off, in Llansteffan,
castle, village and shore
flowered in the marigold sun.
Did those seven men explore
the contrast of this peace
with another English war?

INCENSE (1976) completes a trilogy of volumes with a collection of poems written between 1972 and 1975. It opens with surely the most international of a long tradition of public poems on St David's Day, 'Fanfare for Europe'. This was commissioned by the Arts Council and broadcast from London on Radio 3. It is addressed to an *English* audience, in the magisterial tones of a Welsh spokesman conscious of a long precedence:

Wales went in with Gaul, you see,
with Arthur a late entry.
A couple of milleniums
we've been in.

It welcomes England to the European Union, offers advice:

You're bound to find it strange, new,
unnerving at first, of course –
knowing it only from wars,
power politics, and the brawls
of your French/German royals;

and neatly pips a few other familiar targets –

the imperial bag of tricks . . .
those chimney-pots of fur
on your gratuitous Guards'
heads . . .

What you call pageantry is
merely the war-painted phiz
of Apaches.

It is followed by 'The Poetry of Motion', which conveys the romance of European travel:

To see the Moscow-bound express withdraw
from Amsterdam; imperial, remote,
intent as a risen tsar returning
incognito . . .
And then the Hoek, when the night-boat
slides in at dawn, and all those great
expresses stand – the Lorelei,
the Scandinavie . . .

(the pun is caught this time) before again placing Wales at the centre with one of the volume's many memories of childhood, Degannwy in the 1930s:

But it's the old Welshman *that I recall*
from that steaming railway age . . .
Mr Hughes Stationmaster
in rosebud, neatly furled, and yachting cap
waiting to welcome you (against the lap
of sea on the down platform) in the sails
of his regatta'd speech, home to Wales.

These two poems remind us (by harking back to the European themes of A SENSE OF EUROPE) that this *is* the third volume of a trilogy and emphasize the consistency of Raymond Garlick's life and work – English/Welsh childhood, Wales, Wales-in-Europe. The third poem, 'Trinities', a fine example of making familiar things new, clinches matters with its picture of Trinity College, Carmarthen, as a seat of learning to be set beside Dublin's Trinity and that of Cambridge:

> Within our walls
> the Watkins holograph, the spun
> Gregynog texts, the Rembrandt print.
> Outside, the tree-light of begun
> summer, scarlet fish in the pool,
> the Welsh-poppy flame of the sun.

It is not only the 'Old Ladies' section of this volume which places emphasis on people. 'Llanbadarn Etc' and 'Panegyric' are about, respectively, a contemporary and the real Dafydd ap Gwilym. 'Fern Hill Passed' (the farm is visible from the Llansteffan–Carmarthen road) is another tribute to Dylan Thomas and demonstrates Raymond Garlick's skill (*wide, and innocent, and clear*) at playing off the Saxon against the Romance side of the vocabulary:

> But what an eye was once here –
> wide, and innocent, and clear
> as a rock pool that reflects
> the watcher's face, and perfects
> its own green world with the gold
> of sunlight firing its mould.

The collection contains a tribute to Welsh singers, generous praise of a member of the detested tribe of judges and an exequy for a Roman Catholic bishop. Particularly interesting are the poems which portray members of the poet's family. 'Etching' is a slightly backhanded compliment to his maternal grand-mother, Alice Beere, *her soul, / . . . white and poised as the bowl / of a font*, but her politics monarchist –

> God bless the queen and the British nation
> and teach us to keep our proper station.
> This still passes for education.

'Miss Beatrice' portrays the aunt with whom he shared those memorable childhood experiences of London. 'Encounter' is addressed to a relation of a different kind, God, sensed for the first time in the Catholic church at Pinner:

> I remember opening
> the door of your little house
> in the side-street (it's gone now)
> and slipping soft as a mouse
>
> into the gentle darkness . . .
>
> > the vivid source
> of your being there seemed near
> a small, unwavering flame
> like a heart lit from within.
> I knew you, and said your name.

The unaffected sincerity of this is less remarkable in a poet on the verge of renouncing his religious faith than in another man: Raymond Garlick explains, in 'A Small Boy in the Thirties, II', that his conversion had been an artist's appreciation *of the stately language of Cranmer . . . modes of language* and that maturity taught him that these *were in fact art forms . . . my position had not been belief but make-believe.* This is the last volume in which Catholic faith will drive poetry and its title and concluding section may be seen as a final offering at that altar.

'Adam in Eden' is an unusually physical poem, reminiscent of T. H. Jones in its portrait of the first man:

Down the bronzed plain
a dart of hair
like thickening brush
descends to where

peninsulas
of limbs divide,
sweep into thighs.
And in the wide

and shadowed bay
between those steeps
glazed by the sun
his manhood sleeps.

'Gors Goch' appropriately follows with a flashing glimpse of the Serpent – *their volted coils / sizzling before my feet . . . the vipers drink the heat* – and 'St Anthony's Bay' exemplifies a fallen world in the panic of a rabbit cornered by a ferret. 'Incense', finally, glorifies poetry as service to the Creator.

Praise is what it's all about,
though. Let the exultant shout
of my poem come before
you like incense at the shore
of heaven . . .
Let all be articulate
in the psalm, enter the gate
of words, from being's mute maze
freed. Let the poem shout praise.

Raymond Garlick's candid account, in 'Inspiration and Perspiration', of the drying-up of poetic inspiration, offers a number of explanations: increased creative fulfilment in his teaching; preoccupation with prose-writing; the end of his marriage and the loss of faith which accompanied it; despair about the referendum on devolution, and sheer physical weariness. To these may surely be added the outburst of creativity represented by the three volumes just explored.

It is typical of his orderliness of mind (so well reflected in the orderliness of his writing) that he knew to the day when poetry dried up: 29 August 1979, when he finished the 330-line autobiographical poem, 'Notes for a Biography'. Had this indeed been the final poem, it would have been an appropriate farewell.

The form is six-line (three octosyllabic couplets) stanzas divided into four sections. These explore, respectively, the struggle for independence; education; the Netherlands and Wales; personal and Welsh identity, and the broad message is that if an individual can overcome crippling disability to achieve independence, there is nothing to prevent a nation doing so:

> *My theme's the need to go and meet*
> *Your fate upon your own two feet, . . .*
> *These verses stumble out to try*
> *To stir you into asking why.*

The poem begins with a felicity reminiscent of that of Auden in similar form, the familiar music of rhyme, alliteration, assonance working perfectly. There is no loss of power:

> *More than half spent, the sand-drift*
> *In the hourglass seems to sift*
> *More swiftly.*

How beautifully the vowels sing – *more/half/ drift/*

hour, how well the rhymes (internal and external) are deployed, how effective the alliteration – *spent/sand/seems/sift/swiftly,* how happy the rhythm's play between regularity and variation. This is the mature technique at its best. Perhaps we ought not to expect such art to be sustained, even sustainable throughout a poem of this length – or does one detect (perhaps with hindsight's benefit) a decline as the poem goes on? These lines, for example, are surely trite:

> *There in Holland every day*
> *I found myself obliged to say*
> *Not what I meant but what I could.*
> *But not even to be understood*
> *In your own tongue on your own soil*
> *Must justly make the hot blood boil.*

The first section is a culmination of the line of poems which began with 'Biographical Note':

> *. . . poetry has turned the crutch*
>
> *Of early childhood into form,*
> *Style, structure – letting the warm*
> *Bruised, lacerated living*
> *Of adolescence learn to sing.*
> *Art was the infra-skeleton*
> *The crippled body craved and spun.*

New, however, is a perception of the price we pay for hard-earned autonomy:

> *Pursuit of independence*
> *Works against the social sense.*
> *He who stands on his own two feet*
> *Risks a life that's too complete.*

A life-long wrestle with pain may leave *The exhausted spirit content / Just to tick over, passion spent.* Has it been worthwhile? Of course it has – *Survival is always worth it. / It is our nature . . .*

Section 2 is a modest, humorous self-assessment – he concurs with the university's assessment of his mind *at a lower second* – and an interesting *essay on poetry, writing's highest art*. Poems should be read (*Hearing them is second best*); poetry simple (*If there's need for elucidation / The poem fails to that degree*). Perfection will always be out of reach:

> *The poem lying in wet ink*
> *Upon the page always falls short*
> *Of the perfect poem thought.*
>
> *Art is successful failure . . .*

Section 3 urges Wales to learn, as the poet has, from the Netherlands, *A country on the side of life, to respond / To reasons's sharp-edged diamond . . . / nail the lie / And, like the Dutch, start asking why.* It was in the Netherlands, not Wales, that he learned what it feels like to be *obliged to say / Not what I meant but what I could.* He explores the more complex problem of the Anglo-Welsh:

> *those whose true Welsh mind*
> *Speaks only English have to find*
> *Through English their identity*
> *As Welshmen, their integrity*
> *As citizens.*

and asserts yet again the importance of their tradition:

> For English speech
> As a tongue of Wales stretches the reach
>
> Of centuries: another dress,
> A second weave of Welshness.

The poem's last and longest section returns to the personal:

> an Englishman
> (Ever more English by the year
> It seems) must ask himself: Why here,
> Why Wales, for half a lifetime,
> For a whole life in verse and rhyme?

He hopes that he has *changed / The earth's face slightly*, attacks the concept of *Britishness* (that tool of the incorrigibly imperialist English):

> Be British. Shakespeare
> Wasn't, nor Chaucer, Milton,
> Dafydd ap Gwilym.

and Welshness of the parochial kind:

> Chapel produced a Welsh mind curled
> Round soul, sin, and another world;
> And Rugby's a more recent name
> For turning life into a game;
> Strolling off from reality
> To players' bar or chapel tea.

The English man their own defences, he concludes: who better than an Englishman who has chosen Wales for the sustaining myth of his poetry to lash his adopted countrymen for failing to do as much?

Of the *more than two hundred* poems written between 1946 and 1986, 121 are deemed worthy of preservation in what was designed to be a final volume. Of these the great majority (seventy-three) are taken from the trilogy and only one, four, one and seven respectively from the four earlier volumes. The senior survivor, 'Orchestra', is a tribute to his slightly puzzled lifetime's interest in music. There are more than thirty new poems, presumably composed in the two and a half years between INCENSE and the loss of inspiration.

'Notes for a Biography' is the climax of a series of poems of early life. 'An English Childhood' is about growing up in the thirties and expresses the familiar distaste for suburban London and the English establishment; 'The Rebuttal' rejects the charge (laid over the years by a number of critics) of hating the native land:

> *How*
> *Hate the innocent earth, the hills',*
> *Elgar adagio . . .*
> *Exposed to the heat . . . the invisible ink*
> *Of Englishness indelible showed up.*

'Where?', 'The Art Lesson' and 'The Foxed Mirror' deal with experience at junior and secondary school, 'Tree of Knowledge' (a whimsical pun, for a real tree was involved) with learning the *facts of life* and 'Clock' with his grandmother and great-aunt. Particularly interesting is the series of lyrics which rounds off the volume with an effort to come to terms with the end of marriage and loss of the Catholic faith.

'Wreck' speaks of *Drifting, floating apart . . . She with*

her vivid need / For action . . . He . . . Clinging to flotsam.
Both partners, in different ways, *reached another shore,*
but not, in Raymond Garlick's case, without regret:

> *It was not the young he envied*
> *But the other middle-aged,*
> *The couples moulded by a lifetime's*
> *Bed and board . . .*
>
> ('The Watcher')

'Despoilation' and 'Rites of Passage' lament the end
of religious belief:

> *Year after year he had planted*
> *His feet on those rocks in the stream . . .*
> *He stepped on one that suddenly*
> *Tilted, toppled, threw him in the*
> *Shock of water . . .*

'The Survivor', the most unflinching of the poems
about disability, wonders if all his misfortunes
derive from this:

> *If only penicillin had*
> *Existed then. If only there*
> *Had been some other way to halt*
> *The hamadryad in the blood.*

and 'Beginning Again' in dream-fulfilment retraces
life to the point where

> *he found himself in the park*
> *of early childhood, climbing on*
> *A swing, limbs agile and unflawed.*

There are new poems on familiar themes: Wales,
Europe, what Wales can learn from Europe. The

poems of protest continue with satire of the queen and the judiciary, though these tend now to be slanted towards Welsh apathy:

> *Apart from those in court and gaol*
> *What, then, happened to most of you?*

Emptily neat exercises such as 'Ed White, Astronaut' and 'Ebb Tide', with its trite first stanza, tend to confirm the suggestion of weariness in 'Notes for an Autobiography'. 'Auguries of Guilt', however, is a Blakean indictment of human wickedness:

> *One must be realistic: man*
> *Is crueller and more violent than*
> *All other living creatures . . .*
> *No other animal does this –*
> *Not the hamadryad's kiss*
> *Nor the scorpion's plunging thorn*
> *Match the weapons man has worn.*
> *No cloud of hook-beaked birds of prey*
> *Dismembered Dresden that dark day.*
> *The leopard nor the jaguar*
> *Ripped apart Hiroshima.*

The last two lyrics, taking their cue from the final lines of 'Rites of Passage' (*warmed to the grip of ready / Hands, thrust at once to pull him out*) and 'The Survivor' (*set free the strong, flawed life*) suggest a way forward:

> *Like that lame man, after forty*
> *Years he threw away the crutches*
> *Of his verse and now at last walked*
> *Freely, easily, round the bazaar*
> *Of words.*

('Life Drawing')

83

and

> *From that disturbing night*
> *I twist to this frail now, but*
> *Here I build my hut.*
>
> ('Now and Then')

Life is the one categorical imperative; for as long as we survive, it must be *lived*.

Almost exactly ten years after the urge to write poetry had apparently died, it reasserted itself. As we have seen, Raymond Garlick believes that the decisive stimulus was W. B. Yeats, that great poet whose finest achievement came in his later years. The ten years had not been wasted: there was the continuing fulfilment of teaching (even more enjoyable when, in 1986, it became part-time), the crowning of his work on the Anglo-Welsh tradition by the completion, with Roland Mathias, of what is now the basic textbook, ANGLO-WELSH POETRY, 1480–1980. Increased leisure and the passage of time brought healing and readjustment; a Mediterranean cruise, new inspiration. Most important of all, and most appropriate was

> *the coming of a new generation, being close to the growth of a*
> *new life, which has unsilted the wellsprings of wonder,*
> *tenderness, joy, and confidence in the life-force*
>
> ('A Poet Looks Back')

– the birth of his grandchild, Alys:

> *But why? I think it is the child,*
> *Alys my little grandchild who*
> *In coming has renewed the springs*
> *Of wonder with her life's fresh dew.*

Words flow like tears of tenderness.
Alys, I shape my verse for you.

Raymond Garlick is wont to suggest that the struggle with disability has made him hard, but he is, to use Chaucer's memorable adjective, a *pitous* man. We cannot read these words without recalling, as we are intended to do, those of THE WELSH-SPEAKING SEA, almost forty years previously:

> *For you I make these rhymes that I have run*
> *together, these spare verses I have spun,*
> *to tell you of your riches everywhere.*
> *You shall be happy here, my little son.*

But a Wordsworthian reversal has occurred – this child is father to the poet.

Alys has three poems in the new collection, TRAVEL NOTES (1992), and the poet's Mediterranean cruise twenty-three. Alys's poems are pretty and affectionate, and the Mediterranean's an entertaining mix of human nature and classical reference – youthful, informative, good-humoured. There are poems about Leningrad, Versailles and Lourdes. 'The Commuter' recalls the grandfather to whom the poet owed so much of his interest in words:

> *In velvet-collared overcoat*
> *Buttonholed always with a rose,*
> *Umbrella furled, its ferrule bright*
> *From intervening in the close*
> > *Of Tube train doors, and to rebut*
> > *Their forwardness if they should shut.*

The volume is neatly structured to its title: 'Coming

Home' and 'Here' bring us back from distant parts *into Dyfed, where / Wales opens round the Tywi plain* and *Round the curve from Carmarthen Bay / Into the Tywi's wide embrace* until *I know for sure / My journey's ended. I am here.*

Its first two poems, however, and its concluding one, belong to a different world. 'After George Herbert' is postmodernist in its sustained allusion to 'The Flower'. Starting from Herbert's *Who would have thought my shrivel'd heart / Could have recovered greennesse,* it yokes images together in a manner reminiscent of the Metaphysicals (*The old mine can be opened up, craftsman's tools / Kept honed and oiled, uncorroded as gold*) before returning by way of Herbert's words to the flower / growth image:

> *I once more relish versing. Green*
> *Are the heart's leaves, green as spring,*
> *Green as survival*

and the idea of the refreshing dew and rain of God's mercy. Ironically, not *God*'s mercy at all, the poet no longer believes in a god – it is the child who has *renewed the springs* (how charged *this* phrase is with overtones, among them the fact that creativity returned at the end of the first week of March).

'The Delphic Voyage', longer and more elaborate in form, makes similar allusive patterns out of Yeats's 'Sailing to Byzantium' and, to some degree, out of Keats and Lawrence ('The Ship of Death') also. Remembering the series of poems about how the artifice of poetry compensates for a crippled physique, we cannot be surprised that in old age he should find resonance in Yeats's Byzantium poems.

86

Yeats wrote from the pain of a youthful heart in a failing body; he too found compensation in art. The diction and tone of Raymond Garlick's poem are deceptively simple after Yeats's measured rhetoric – *The cabin's booked, the passage paid* – but the preoccupations are similar:

> It's time. An aging man must nail
> His tatters to the mast, Yeats said,
> And take ship in the creaking, frail
> Hull of his life, and seek to come
> Before he dies to Byzantium.

Having removed from his COLLECTED POEMS everything of Catholic inspiration, he refrains from calling the city holy and indeed the poem ends with him still on his way. This journey is not to Byzantium at all, but to Parnassus, and its end is to find a faith there. The death of the oracle is a comfort:

> No priest or imam there to cry
> Vengeance or guilt, urge men to shed
> Each other's blood for some contrived
> And bitter god inside the head.

Natural beauty and man's achievement are accorded equal validity: this place *Where crimson poppies hang in bud* bears also *monuments / Of man's magnificence* and if there *is* a deity acceptable by a reasonable man, *Lyric Apollo might be the one.*

These are two of, perhaps *the two* finest poems that Raymond Garlick has written, and they are more complex and allusive than his earlier work. After the easier, but always entertaining, interesting and well crafted travel poems, the volume closes with 'The

Odyssey Continues' (a title which refers us back to the *Ghost-galleys of Odysseus* in 'The Delphic Voyage'). It begins with Browning's *We mortals cross the ocean of / This world, each in his average / Cabin of a life*, and the image is sustained with *bone-cage of a cabin* (the compound noun is pure Saxon – *ban-hus*), *shipwrecked, sheltered, members of the crew*, to the conclusion. Homer and Browning are joined by Yeats – *high Byzantium of art*. The poem asserts that lost faith, like physical disability, has been compensated for by art, lost marriage by loving children, a grandchild and good friends:

> *Half the happiness of my life*
> *Comes through a son, the other through*
> *A daughter. Now, warm harbinger*
> *Of poetry, there's Alys too:*
> *These, and many an outstretched hand*
> *Of friendship, keep this cabin manned.*

Art and life are combined once more in the memorable conclusion:

> *The high Byzantium of art,*
>   *Led by dolphins and white sea-birds*
>   *Leaping and fluttering like words.*

This poet's sea is *dolphin-torn*, but not *gong-tormented*; there is no suggestion here of *blood-dimmed tide* or reeling *shadows of indignant desert birds*.

'A Poet Looks Back' notes the irony – a double one as it turned out – of a review of COLLECTED POEMS 1946–86:

I was wryly moved by a review in the TIMES LITERARY SUPPLEMENT *which said of some of the contents that they hold, at a late stage in a career, promises of future development.*

The review's inadvertent prescience which hindsight has enabled us to confirm should be a warning (if Yeats and Hardy are not warning enough) that ageism is no more acceptable in literary criticism than anywhere else.

III

It remains to consider Raymond Garlick's achievement as editor, critic and prose-writer, in particular his crucial role in the recognition of Anglo-Welsh writing as a genre dating from the fifteenth century. His clarity of mind and pertinacity of purpose have been extremely influential in securing its cultural and educational acceptance in Wales (school, college and university syllabuses; WJEC examinations; the setting up of the Universities of Wales Association for the Study of Welsh Writing in English) and its critical and scholarly recognition throughout the world. His gifted teaching, in secondary schools and at Trinity College, Carmarthen, has been an essential part of the process – it is time for the academic establishment to recognize that teaching too is scholarship and criticism – and we have already noted that the initial challenge of teaching literature in English to Welsh children was extremely important.

There is no need to recapitulate the arguments which have been rehearsed, since the 1930s at least, by Welsh writers, Welsh writers in English, and, too often acrimoniously, between the two on this no longer contentious subject. It *is* worth mentioning the contribution of A. G. Prys-Jones as anthologist, poet and critic: his complete self-confidence as a Welshman writing in English (not unconnected with the fact that he was Welsh-speaking) did much to prepare the way and, unlike some supporters of the tradition, he did not feel obliged to be apologetic about it. Raymond Garlick, an Englishman and a poet for whom Wales-as-myth was a conscious choice, had the advantage of an outsider's perspective. His early and warm friendships with Welsh writers were no less essential a qualification – it is no accident that Saunders Lewis, for example, was a subscriber and contributor to DOCK LEAVES from an early stage.

Addressing the Universities of Wales Association for the Study of Welsh Writing in English in March 1993, Raymond Garlick remembered how, in 1944, Keidrych Rhys's anthology had made him aware of an *indefinable distinctiveness* in the work of Welsh people writing in English and uneasy that *the frame of reference in which Anglo-Welsh poetry is seen* [was] *British Anglo-American*. This led him, as editor of DOCK LEAVES:

> *to begin to wonder whether a different kind of context, that of Wales, Welsh literature, and the past experience of English as a language of Wales, might not prove more appropriate and illuminating. My concern was never to fit Anglo-Welsh writing into a London/English literature context, but to discover what was different and distinctive about it.*

A similar problem has, in more recent years, been faced by writers in former English colonies – Chinua Achebe responds to it in his essay 'Colonialist Criticism' with:

> *Let no one be fooled by the fact that we may write in English for we intend to do unheard of things with it.*

DOCK LEAVES was founded in 1949 by

> *a group of writers living in the southern part of Pembrokeshire and meeting at regular intervals to discuss their craft and art.*

91

The initiative came from Roland Mathias, recently installed headmaster of Pembroke Dock County School, and it was natural that Raymond Garlick, just appointed as a teacher of English, should act as editor. The group, *probably never more than a dozen at any one time*, would meet informally once a month. The first issue, Christmas 1949, comprises thirty-one pages and contains the work of seven individuals: Roland Mathias, Raymond Garlick, Olwyn Rees, Nora E. Davies, Morwyth Rees, L. Alun Page and C. C. Read. It contains twenty poems, three short stories and an article on 'The World of T. S. Eliot'. The second issue contains the earliest significant editorial (on Welsh nationality) and introduces visual art (an article by Arthur Giardelli), illustrations (in the form of small, attractive engravings) and book reviews, one of them by Glyn Jones. Number 3 is the first with a European dimension (an account of the Garlicks' pilgrimage to Rome) and brings in Welsh writing with an essay on T. Gwynn Jones. A piece on William Morris shows how far the range has already been extended. Number 5 recognizes a significant new poet, T. H. Jones. Soon music, the Welsh language, education, politics, history, sociology and broadcasting will complete the range. Photographs are introduced in Number 13, 'A Dylan Thomas Number', which is the first to be devoted to a single topic. With Number 23, 1957, Raymond Garlick significantly altered the title to THE ANGLO-WELSH REVIEW, the name 'Dock Leaves' being reserved for the Press. There were now a hundred pages, four pages of photographs, twenty-three contributors and the subjects covered included music, painting and cinema. It was an enormous achievement, for the periodical was maintained by the voluntary fund-raising activities of a small group, and a number of apparently better found literary magazines had failed during the period.

Raymond Garlick continued as editor until Number 26 (1960), publishing work by or about more than 180 individuals, including such notable Welsh writers as Saunders Lewis, D. J. Williams, Waldo Williams, 'Crwys', 'Trefin', 'Cynan', Aneirin Talfan, Pennar Davies, Tecwyn Lloyd, Islwyn Ffowc Elis, Dilys Cadwaladr, Dyfnallt Morgan, Bobi Jones and R. Gerallt Jones. His editorials and reviews, even more than the work he published, demonstrate his progress as scholar and critic and the development of the theory which was to achieve its full statement in AN INTRODUCTION TO ANGLO-WELSH LITERATURE (1970, revised 1972) and the anthology ANGLO-WELSH POETRY 1480–1980 (1984, revised 1993). In Number 2, Easter 1950, he is already laying the groundwork with a significant discussion of Welsh nationality:

What is it, in short, that makes a nation – is it language? . . . More than half the population of Wales does not speak the Welsh language . . . Participation in a literature and culture . . . is insufficient ground for nationality . . . Ultimately a man is of a certain nationality because he wills it so . . .

In Numbers 4 and 5 there is a vigorous defence of the National Eisteddfod:

those who object to the National Eisteddfod in its present form should either direct their energies to learning the language, or have an eisteddfod of their own somewhere else . . . The living capital of Wales is still the travelling capital of the National Eisteddfod, where cultural autonomy at least is fittingly lodged.

The question of Anglo-Welsh writing is sceptically addressed in Number 6 (Michaelmas 1951). Stimulated by a *treasure* of *literary criticism* from an anti-Home-Rule MP: *The soul of Wales is finding expression in the writings of the Anglo-Welsh school of poets and authors*, the young editor emphatically declares that:

there is no such thing as a school *of Anglo-Welsh writers . . . there is, as yet, no appreciable tradition . . . Anglo-Welsh writing, if we except the handful of Welshmen who have chosen to express themselves in English during the last four hundred years, is a child almost of our own times.*

In 1952, Ioan Bowen Rees ('Wales and the Anglo-Welsh'), wrote: *The Anglo-Welsh have . . . no long tradition of speaking English while remaining Welsh,* and Raymond Garlick saw no reason to disagree:

With four departments of English flourishing in the University of Wales, I assumed (as a recent graduate of one of them) that any evidence of an opposite tendency – of a considerable number of Welshmen of earlier times writing poetry or prose in English, but out of the experience of being Welsh – would have been uncovered long since.

He was less confident than his assertiveness suggested: in Number 7 (Spring 1952) he moves from a complaint that so few Welsh grammar school libraries include the works of Hopkins, Edward Thomas, W. H. Davies and Wilfred Owen, let alone those of Alun Lewis, Huw Menai, R. S. Thomas, Idris Davies and Vernon Watkins, to the hope

that someone will persuade a publishing house to put forth a badly-needed anthology of Anglo-Welsh poetry from the seventeenth century to the twentieth, such as might find a place upon the Grammar School syllabus . . .

He goes on to criticize the University of Wales, for providing:

94

a provincial English education . . . the University has almost completely neglected even those Welsh poets and novelists who write in that English tongue which it has selected as its medium of teaching, administration, and corporate life. Where . . . is the long-overdue critical study of the influence of Welsh poets in English upon the whole course of English poetry – that influence, so potent and fruitful, which began in the seventeenth century . . . Only one who has the freedom of libraries and the time and facilities at the disposal of a research scholar can attempt the task . . . how many of these poets were Welsh-speaking? how many had at least a second-hand acquaintance with cynghanedd*? . . . a section at least of this large field of study is now being investigated in one of the American universities, and the University of Algiers has recently proposed the poetry of Dylan Thomas as the subject for a degree dissertation.*

The University would continue (and through its powerful influence on the WJEC ensure that that body continued) to resist the recognition of the Anglo-Welsh tradition until the Association for the Study of Welsh Writing in English was established in 1985.

In spite of shortage of time and facilities, Raymond Garlick resolved to attempt the research himself:

I decided to establish as conclusively as I could that such evidence as there was led inevitably to the accepted judgements . . . I would show that the English language was of such recent provenance in Wales that its creative use by Welshmen was more or less a twentieth century phenomenon: and thus that an Anglo-Welsh Literature could not yet exist. Inductively I would demonstrate that, before the present century, only a handful of writers – of dubious Welshness – had in fact produced poetry and prose in English: and thus that an Anglo-Welsh Literature did not yet exist.

(AN INTRODUCTION TO ANGLO-WELSH LITERATURE)

Number 11 (Summer 1953) compares Anglo-Welsh

with Anglo-Irish writing and suggests that the former is *possibly of more ancient origin.* The year 1521, which saw the *first book by a Welshman to be printed,* the Abridgement of the Common Law by William Owen, is suggested as an approximate starting-date and there is the outline of the historical background from Norman times. The accession of Henry Tudor, the twentieth provision of the Act of Union of Henry VIII and the establishment of the Tudor grammar schools and of Jesus College, Oxford are put forward as decisive events.

By 1954 Raymond Garlick had managed a good deal of informal research. In 1953 he had presented a paper to the Dock Leaves Group and their criticism, particularly Roland Mathias's contribution, had enabled him to clarify his view. The Dublin Magazine (January–March 1954) published 'Anglo-Welsh Poetry from 1587 to 1800' and the Welsh Anvil (Vol. VI, December 1954) 'Seventy Anglo-Welsh Poets'. The latter advances six general propositions which form the foundation of his thesis:

1. *That from the accession of Henry Tudor, in 1485, onwards English became one of the languages (in some cases the only language) of numbers of Welshmen.*
2. *That this tendency to use English was stimulated by the language policy of Henry VIII's Act of Union of 1535 (especially by its twentieth provision), by the change of religion, and by the establishment of the Tudor Grammar Schools and of Jesus College, Oxford.*
3. *That the persons most affected by these – the gentry and Anglican clergy – possessed two of the pre-requisites, literacy in English and leisure, for the creation of a new literature.*
4. *That the literature they created, if any, would for long be one written by a minority for a minority, so far as Wales was concerned.*

5. That this would not of itself invalidate the literature as a literature of Wales, since literature in Welsh in our own day is created by a minority for a minority.
6. That literature in English is not necessarily the same thing as the literature of England (upon the analogy of the American, Scots, South African and other national literatures in English).

There follows a list of seventy-one Anglo-Welsh poets, beginning with Morris Kyffin (1555–98), twenty-eight of them Welsh-speaking and seventeen who wrote poetry in Welsh. All seventy-one *have in common an ancestry of great antiquity.* The tradition is defined: *an extensive and distinctive minor poetry for the most part, moving towards a major poetry in our own day* [with] *Dylan Thomas.* Three general characteristics are traced: *a preoccupation with form . . . a metaphysical interest . . . a line of topographical poetry* beginning *with Dyer.*

'Anglo Welsh Poetry from 1587 to 1800', elegant and forceful, opens with further criticism of the University:

The field is not merely virgin but is likely to remain permanently in that condition so far as Welsh scholarship is concerned, the official attitude of the University of Wales being that there is insufficient material in the subject for it to be acceptable in a thesis title.

It identifies Swrdwal's 'Hymn to the Virgin' as the first poem in English by a Welshman and suggests that *the continuous line of Anglo-Welsh poets seems to begin with Morris Kyffin, who was born about 1555.* The accepted view is described as *wholly untenable*:

the second literature of Wales is all but coeval with the second language; . . . English, at least as a second language, became generally spoken by certain classes of Welshmen from 1485 . . . onwards; . . . from Morris Kyffin (c. 1555/1598) to Idris Davies . . . there have been at least sixty-five Anglo-Welsh poets . . .

Anglo-Welsh poetry is defined as *poetry written in the English language by Welshmen* and a Welsh person is defined, as at the National Eisteddfod, as *A person born in Wales, or of Welsh parents . . . or any person able to speak or write the Welsh language.*

The flocking to London of large numbers of Welshmen as a result of the accession of Henry VII is explored, together with the Act of Union and the founding of English-speaking grammar schools and Jesus College, Oxford. He points out that significant contemporary figures – A. G. Prys-Jones, Huw Menai, R. S. Thomas, Glyn Jones and Emyr Humphreys – are Welsh-speaking. Each of the *general propositions* is more fully explored, and there are quotations from Morgan Llwyd, Evan Evans (Ieuan Brydydd Hir), Edward Davies and Richard Llwyd. Particularly interesting are the suggestions that the Metaphysical tradition owes its origin to Wales and that Anglo-Welsh poets, from Donne to Dylan Thomas, derive their preoccupation with form from *classical poetry in the Welsh language.*

Having to his own satisfaction established the reality of the Anglo-Welsh genre, Raymond Garlick devoted himself to its recognition in its homeland. Number 23, the first under the title ANGLO-WELSH REVIEW, celebrates the fact that

during the lifetime of DOCK LEAVES the term has . . . become respectable common-usage – on the wireless, in newspapers, and in literary periodicals at home and abroad. With its unsensational appearance [June 1956] *in the pages of the* TIMES LITERARY SUPPLEMENT, *that court-circular of the literatures of the English language, its propriety might have seemed at last to be above reproach.*

The award of an honorary doctorate to Richard Hughes is noted with pleasure and the *palace revolution* of Professor Gwyn Jones's lecture, 'The First Forty Years: Some Notes on Anglo-Welsh Literature', on 8 February 1957, and its subsequent publication by the University of Wales Press is praised.

The Educational Establishment is not – the University has failed to encourage scholarship; neither at University nor Training College level do syllabuses recognize the Anglo-Welsh tradition:

So long as the Anglo-Welsh tradition is ignored, so long will the teaching of English in the schools – whether as a first or as a second language – lack integrity. The extent of this failure may be measured by the fact that no kind of book designed for school use – whether anthology of poetry or prose, or literary or linguistic history – yet exists.

Number 24, essentially a review of R. S. Thomas's POETRY FOR SUPPER, stresses the interdependence of Welsh and Anglo-Welsh writing; Number 25, reviewing Gwyn Williams's anthology, PRESENTING WELSH POETRY, congratulates author and publisher on *being the first to make a foray into this hitherto unrepresented hinterland of Anglo-Welsh poetry,* and notes that *during these last ten years . . . Anglo-Welsh writing has become regarded as a literature.* Significant academic progress is recorded:

The University of Wales has awarded a research degree for a thesis on Idris Davies, and the Sorbonne has accepted a diploma on Dylan Thomas . . . Of the Colleges, several have Anglo-Welsh Societies and one has recently established an Alun Lewis Society. There has been a summer school on the Anglo-Welsh at Coleg Harlech. Last year the magazine WALES resumed publication . . . and this year the Third Programme has put out an elusive symposium on the Anglo-Welsh.

Number 26, Raymond Garlick's final word as editor, takes a gloomier view: contemporary Welsh literature is in a healthy condition, but there is a shortage of young Welsh writers in English. Welsh secondary education is criticized (*rarely a Welsh secondary education at all, but only a provincial one*) and the difficulty of finding a publisher identified:

The Anglo-Welsh writer . . . is excluded by his very nature – by the English publisher because he is too closely Welsh, and by the Welsh publisher because he writes in English.

His decision to return to Wales and his work at Trinity College, notably as Director of Welsh Studies, together with his very practical contribution as a member of the Literature Committee of the Welsh Arts Council, have already been referred to. It was his active encouragement and help which enabled W. Randal Jenkins and myself to produce the two teaching anthologies, TWELVE MODERN ANGLO-WELSH POETS (for secondary schools and colleges) and WALES TODAY (for primary schools).

In 1922 H. Idris Bell had referred to *the poets of what I may call the Anglo-Welsh movement* and suggested that *there may hereafter arise a poet to do for Anglo-Welsh literature what W. B. Yeats has done for*

100

Anglo-Irish. In 1970 Raymond Garlick completed his work on the tradition with AN INTRODUCTION TO ANGLO-WELSH LITERATURE. An early reference to Bell is apposite in more ways than one:

It is perhaps appropriate that the term and concept Anglo-Welsh, in its literary application, should have been launched upon its course in the twentieth century by an Englishman devoted to Wales, to Welsh Literature, and to the attempt to convey something of its life through translation into English.

and he employs the words of R. S. Thomas, the poet who has fulfilled Bell's prophecy, to underline the distinction between English literature and literature written in English: *Despite our speech we are not English: most Anglo-Welsh writers would endorse R. S. Thomas's line.*

In AN INTRODUCTION TO ANGLO-WELSH LITERATURE the development of Welsh literature in English is traced from the Statute of Rhuddlan (1284) to the first half of the twentieth century (Jack Jones, Wyn Griffith, David Jones and A. G. Prys-Jones, all of them alive at the time this book was written) and, in terms of anthologies, to THE LILTING HOUSE (1969). No attempt is made to deal with contemporary Anglo-Welsh writing, and the essay concludes with brief biographical and bibliographical details of sixty-nine writers from Ieuan ap Hywel Swrdwal (fl. 1430–80) to T. H. Jones (1921–65).

In its beginnings, and for much of its history, Anglo-Welsh writing was the work of bilingual writers. To this day, it has been written with an awareness of the Welsh language and, in the case of poetry, often of the formal techniques of Welsh verse. The force of this is made clear by the position of Dylan Thomas, about whom *some Anglo-American criticism* makes the assumption that his poetry *might as easily have been composed in Swanage or Sewanee as in Swansea*. Raymond Garlick shows that Thomas was *aware of an Anglo-Welsh Literature* and saw himself *as a part of it*. His:

> *virtuoso* craft or art, *characteristic of Anglo-Welsh poetry from the beginning; its use of* proest, cymeriadau, *modified* cynghanedd: *its topography, and the allusions that derive from it (the larger-than-life* MABINOGI *in the tall tales / Beyond the border of Pembrokeshire, across which the road from Laugharne leads up to Narberth): all these illuminate the observation in* THE TIMES *obituary (written by Vernon Watkins) that it was, even in its first phases, an ancient poetry, not rejecting antiquity for the present but seeking, with every device of language, the ancestry of the moment.*

Another contention and one which Raymond Garlick would apply to all Anglo-Welsh writing is expressed in T. S. Eliot's words:

> *His significance, his appreciation is the appreciation of his relation to the dead poets and artists. You cannot value him alone: you must set him, for comparison and contrast, among the dead.* ('Tradition and the Individual Talent')

Throughout the essay, themes are identified and traced, connections made. John Davies (*c.* 1565–1618)

> *is articulating for the first time one of the roles of the Anglo-Welsh poet – the interpretative – in which he speaks to an outside audience who know little or nothing of Wales.*

John Dyer (1699–1757) is one of the first poets to show clearly the *sense of what Eliot has called* a particular people in a particular place:

it is in the eighteenth century that Welsh landscape emerges as one of the major themes of Anglo-Welsh poetry.

John Stuart Williams and Dylan Thomas are quoted as modern examples, and it is suggested that

All the Anglo-Welsh landscape poems of the eighteenth century embody the two qualities of Welsh landscape which form the theme of R. S. Thomas's poem of that title – 'the past, / Brittle with relics' and the sense of desolation.

The same poet's 'Welsh History' is used to introduce the theme of the past as triumphant and golden, the confidence of *an old and haughty Nation proud in Arms* that *they are the top people.* Comparing Edward Davies's 'Chepstow' with R. S. Thomas's poem, Garlick finds that

Both depict a ragged forefather of Iago Prytherch, but Davies's peasant is magnificently contemptuous of the judgements and pretensions of others.

Although the main preoccupation is with a *poetic* tradition, prose is not ignored. The first example is the Abridgement of the Common Law (1521) of William Owen of Henllys in Pembrokeshire, *the first book by a Welshman to be printed.* Morgan Llwyd (1619–59) and Dom Augustine Baker (1575–1641) are mentioned as landmark figures, the latter's Holy Wisdom (1657) *a classic of the contemplative life.* Notable letter-writers are mentioned; autobiography is said to have begun with Herbert of Cherbury; antiquarian and topographical writing *descends from George Owen of Henllys (1552–1613).*

It is important to remember that AN INTRODUCTION TO ANGLO-WELSH LITERATURE *is* no more than that. Raymond Garlick warns us (with characteristic modesty) that:

The present essay consists of an outline of material that has come to light . . . over the last sixteen years . . . compiled without benefit of library, or research procedures; it has been taken from secondary, printed sources . . . I could have wished that the poets might have been served with scholarship, instead of merely with affection.

It concludes with three suggestions which are worth repeating: that

the view that sees the Welsh language and its culture as the acropolis of most that is best in the past and present of Wales – does not in the least depend upon the denigration of Anglo-Welsh literature; [that] *some literary pleasure is to be got from these writers of the centuries before our own, 'minute objects in the landscape' though (in Eliot's words) some of them may be; that the social and educational function of Anglo-Welsh Literature in contemporary Wales* [must, in bilingual education and a bilingual society] *be to present the two languages and cultures as complementary.*

A great deal of work is now being done, principally through the Universities of Wales Association for the Study of Welsh Writing in English whose annual, Gregynog colloquia provide focus and publicity. It is a pity that Raymond Garlick never found time to revise his essay in the light of his work at Trinity College, where both library and research procedures *were* available to him. In any event, it must form the basis for the scholar who, surely in the near future, will compile the first HISTORY OF ANGLO-WELSH LITERATURE.

One more critical work merits brief consideration, if only to give a perspective to Raymond Garlick's disingenuity (a source of amusement to those who were privileged to conduct the seminars which he devised) about his scholarly and critical skills – the essay 'The Shapes of Thoughts' (POETRY WALES, Autumn 1973). Its purpose is to give a detailed *reading* of what he calls *Dylan Thomas's 'Ode on the Morning of Christ's Nativity'*, 'Vision and Prayer'. The reason for the poem's extreme complexity (its *welcome obstacles* in the words of Professor Walford Davies) is defined by a quotation from Donne: *I thought, if I could draw my paines, / Through Rimes vexation, I should them allay* and its form related to the work of Herbert:

To the reader of the Anglo-Welsh poetry of the past, the best known shapes of thoughts left by the dead are likely to be George Herbert's poems 'The Altar' and 'Easter Wings'.

A poet, Raymond Garlick continues,

may deliberately set himself the vexing problem of a complicated syllabic and rhyming shape, partly for the pleasure of exercising all his technical skills to solve it, but primarily because he is aware that this is the only way in which he can contain certain strong emotions and transform them into art.

There follows an account of the *strong emotions* that require the control of: 204 lines arranged in twelve stanzas of seventeen lines each; the first six stanzas having the syllabic pattern of 12345678987654321 per line, the second 98765432123456789; an intricate pattern of end-rhyming, consonantal and assonantal rhyme and the rhyming of accented with unaccented syllables; alliteration both within and across lines.

The VISION is clearly of a birth, turning to a death; the PRAYER is equally clearly that there may be no resurrection, and the prayer fails triumphantly in the final stanza. The poem is, in short, about the birth of light, the darkness of death, the unbearable effulgence of resurrection . . . The quality of violent personal experience, of cataclysm, turmoil and upheaval, is emphasised by minimum punctuation, and the containing role of the poem's shape becomes apparent.

This broad explanation is followed by detailed exposition which, in range, depth, precision and resourcefulness, demonstrates critical scholarship of a high order. Added to the editorials, reviews, critical essays, the anthology and the INTRODUCTION, it suggests that Raymond Garlick's deprecation of his lack of postgraduate qualifications and university teaching experience is misplaced.

I have quoted at such length from the non-critical prose that there is little that needs to be said of it here. From university days (we remember the publication of student essays in literary journals) he has written with an ease that is the unmistakable sign of meticulous craftsmanship. The style is elegant, concise and humane, in the central tradition of the best English prose. He has an unerring sense of decorum. The wit which has enlivened virtually everything that he has written is usually gentle, often self-deprecating, but he can rise to Johnsonian heights when suitably provoked. He is adept, as the latest biographical essays show, at the presentation of character.

IV

Raymond Garlick's most important achievement is, of course, his poetry. As early as 1955, A. G. Prys-Jones, reviewing THE WELSH-SPEAKING Sea, referred to *meticulous craftsmanship, alliteration and assonance used to fine effect, a passionate love of Wales, its language and traditions.* No later critic has seriously dissented from this assessment. Glyn Jones and John Rowlands, in PROFILES (Gomer Press, 1980), praise *sincerity of feeling and unfaltering technical skill*, relate his work specifically to the Welsh tradition:

he frequently uses traethodl, *which is a sort of cywydd without the cynghanedd, which permits rhymes other than accented syllable with unaccented*

(Raymond Garlick says he finds this an *interesting and haunting* measure) and point to *poems about people* which are *in the old Welsh tradition, poems of celebration and praise.*

Roland Mathias (ANGLO-WELSH REVIEW, 41) points to another quality which we have seen to be present from the beginning – *There never was a time . . . when he was without a sense of Europe*, and Jeremy Hooker (POETRY WALES 8,4) sums up the achievement, in general terms, with:

A major poet extending the tradition that his own writings have done so much to bring to our attention.

The most interesting assessments, however, are those

of Tony Bianchi (PLANET 40, 1977) and Tony Conran and Leslie Norris (NEW WELSH REVIEW, 1988). Tony Bianchi's challenging 'Let the Poem Show Praise' echoes the above reference to *poems of celebration and praise*. Although technically a review of INCENSE, it is in fact a wide-ranging exploration of the nature of the poet's work, his inspiration and development.

Tony Bianchi concludes that Raymond Garlick is *among Wales's most versatile and accomplished poetic craftsmen* and recognizes his concern with integration *firstly of the self, and then . . . of the self's role in the public world*. He identifies the

zealous regard for the continuity of literary traditions . . . comparable with Eliot's two great Welsh disciples – Saunders Lewis and David Jones . . . in his cherishing of ancient cultural traditions and his manipulating of parallels and continuities between different historical phases.

He disparages, however, the

elevation of the slim Anglo-Welsh contribution to Welsh letters over the last three centuries to the level of a tradition parallel and compatible with the Welsh language contribution, however inferior to it in status

(thereby hinting at the kind of animosity that Raymond Garlick, throughout his career, had gone out of his way to avoid) and refers to

Garlick's historicist defence of the Anglo-Welsh writer's role as by now a dead horse, well flogged and no longer of much interest to the poet himself.

Tony Bianchi believes that at the centre of Raymond

108

Garlick's inspiration is an aestheticist's tendency to prefer the image to the reality, that

he is not really talking about history, or Europe, or Wales at all . . . the past has always appeared to be a buttress with which to support himself.

The commitment to Wales is seen as *partly explicable by his bitter dislike of his native . . . England,* and there is a reference to *strange ostrich posturings.* When he goes on to claim that the choice for the Anglo-Welsh writer is between identification with the Welsh-speaking community and a flight into the fantasy of some ideal Wales of the imagination, it is evident that he has misunderstood both the man and the poet. An English poet who has, consciously even at the time, spent the happiest days of his childhood in Welsh-speaking Wales, living with close relations themselves fully committed to their Welsh community, who has relished his secondary and higher education in Welsh-speaking Wales, who has married a Welsh-speaker, learned the language and numbers Welsh writers amongst his best and earliest friends, is hardly likely to require or suffer from such illusions or need to practise such self-deception. That a poet may make a nation the myth for some, or all of his best poetry without having any illusions about it is as evident in Raymond Garlick's work as it is in that of W. B. Yeats and R. S. Thomas. His marriage of himself and his art to Wales certainly began with love at first sight, but, like all enduring relationships, it is founded on quotidian realities.

The first 'movement' ('One, the Shadow') of Tony Conran's beautiful 'Symphony in 3 Movements', ALL HALLOWS (Gomer Press, 1995), pays generous poetic tribute to his *Precise dreamer* friend:

109

A kind, principled outsider
In Wales, gradually
Rooting in the green and white
Peace that you wanted. Teacher
Of peace . . .

('Curriculum Vitae')

In 1988 both he and Leslie Norris, writing in response to COLLECTED POEMS 1946–1986, noted the effect of the departure from chronological order, the latter pointing to the interesting juxtapositions which result and the former developing a serious and much more fundamental point – the censoring out of Catholicism. Tony Conran traces *a gradual loosening of his imagination from the ties of ideology* which gave the early work the *characteristic* frisson *of a cultural fetishist* and notes that the move to the Netherlands in 1960 produced *a much greater emphasis on moral and political point-making* and *an air of armchair pontificating.* Echoing Tony Bianchi, he suggests that:

Like many Englishmen who come here, he looked for peace and quality of life – respectable, literary, moral values

but he gives the poet credit for adapting his vision to *the tragic peripeteia* of the period of civil disobedience (though he cannot really forgive him for the adaptation of his Catholicism to reality).

For Tony Conran, *his religion makes him a better poet than he would otherwise have been* and it does not matter to the reader *whether his experience was or was not of a genuine supernatural order.* Tony Conran's favourite collection is A SENSE OF TIME, and he makes a very persuasive point about the *poems of outrage*:

As these poems were originally collected . . . the outrage was

*only part of an imaginative vision of what happened in the
streets and lawcourts of Swansea; part of something greater,
part of God's dealing with the world, part of the order of love:
martyrdom and finding, suffering and glory, pacifism and the
Cross. It's that dimension . . . that makes the book a
contribution to tragic vision.*

I do not see how one can be unsympathetic to this
view. We remember how Auden censored the
political commitment out of his early poems –
though, more pragmatic or less honest than
Raymond Garlick, he reprinted some of them in their
gelded form. It is certainly much more convenient
for the critic to have the poetry chronologically
before him; equally, it is certainly too much to expect
the poet to reprint work in which he has lost faith.
Perhaps the fairest adjudication is that Tony Conran
is right because poems are not autobiographies and,
irrespective (even) of the poet's later view of the
authenticity of his ideology at the time of
composition, must stand for the reader as the
arrangement of words, the deployment of images
that is all they truly are – but Raymond Garlick is
right too, because a poet (particularly a *lyric* poet)
must write out of what he feels in the contemporary
moment and to do so may have to shake from his
neck the albatross of his past.

I conclude with Leslie Norris because his perception
of Raymond Garlick so nearly coincides with my
own. He emphasizes first that *stern regard for high
quality* (about which there has never been critical
disagreement) and *that realistic modesty which is one of
his most endearing personal attributes*. He notes the
admirable clarity of the poetry, the reserved nature of
the man, his personal formality and meticulousness,

the combination of *detachment and outright honesty* which makes poems such as 'Biographical Note' and 'Indirect Speech' *necessary to an understanding of the rest of the work*. He would disagree with Tony Conran, for he sees Raymond Garlick as *keeping faithful to early principles and applying them to whatever new experiences came his way*. He qualifies the poet's relationship to the work of Welsh-born writers by suggesting that his poetry lacks *that element of mystery which we in Wales think an almost essential quality of the best poetry* – and thus encourages us to consider again a clarity reminiscent of the Augustans, in particular Pope, with whom Raymond Garlick has a good deal more than disability in common.

Leslie Norris's conclusion is so just that I conclude by quoting it in full:

We owe Raymond Garlick a debt of gratitude, not only for his devoted service to poetry in general, to Anglo-Welsh poetry in particular, or to Wales. An Englishman (his poems [his most recent publications allow us to add his prose work] *about his English childhood are delightful), he has served us well. His scholarship, of which there are many evidences . . . has been unsparingly used in the cause of his adopted country. Yet he remains, as he says himself, '. . . an Englishman / (Ever more English by the year / It seems)' . . . Garlick does not deny his history, nor his humanity . . . A serious, honest, concerned and civilised man, he brings those virtues to his poetry.*

V

At the age of fifteen and a half, Raymond Garlick was obliged to accept

that the whole of life was to be lived in a crippled mode; that symmetry of physique, physical achievement, grace and ease of movement, were forever unattainable.

As soon as he had recovered from the consequent breakdown, he set about achieving in art all that appeared impossible in life. Artistic creation alone can shape the inchoate into coherence, transform life's temporary agonies into eternal, consoling beauty. The first of his unflinching biographical poems, written in his twenties, defined his intention, expressed his need:

As earth desires the rain, the womb the seed, pain
Rest, conception birth, the burning lover
His beloved's breast: just so, to pin

A syntax on existence and to voice
The vowels of being is the hot desire
Locked in my knotted limbs and body's vice.

It is not merely the words – the elegant, balanced prose as well as the poetry and the pertinacious proselytizing for Wales and Anglo-Welsh literature – but the whole of his life that has been transformed by the process of artistic creation: the voice, modulated in conversation and in teaching, the manner, manners, decorum, the self-deprecating humour. Of all the artists I know, W. B. Yeats best understands the poet's imperative need to remake himself and best conveys, in the immortal image of 'Byzantium', a sense of Raymond Garlick's achievement:

> *Once out of nature I shall never take*
> *My bodily form from any natural thing,*
> *But such a form as Grecian goldsmiths make*
>
> *Of hammered gold and gold enamelling . . .*

Bibliography

RAYMOND GARLICK

Poetry

POEMS MCMXLVII (with Louis Olav Leroi), privately printed, 1946.

POEMS FROM THE MOUNTAIN-HOUSE, London, The Fortune Press, 1950.

THE WELSH-SPEAKING SEA (SELECTED POEMS 1949–1954), Tenby, Dock Leaves Press, 1954.

REQUIEM FOR A POET, Tenby, Dock Leaves Press, 1954 (Dock Leaves Pamphlet: 1).

POEMS FROM PEMBROKESHIRE, Tenby, Dock Leaves Press, 1954 (Dock Leaves Pamphlet: 2).

BLAENAU OBSERVED, A BROADCAST POEM, Tenby, Dock Leaves Press, 1957. (Broadcast on the BBC Welsh Home Service on 14 June 1956.)

LANDSCAPES AND FIGURES (Selected Poems), London, Merrythought Press, 1964 (limited edition).

A SENSE OF EUROPE (Collected Poems 1954–1968), Llandysul, Gomer Press, 1968.

A SENSE OF TIME (Poems and Antipoems 1969–1972), Llandysul, Gomer Press, 1972.

INCENSE (Poems 1972–75), Llandysul, Gomer Press, 1976.

THE HYMN TO THE VIRGIN (Attributed to Ieuan ap Hywel Swrdwal, with an Introduction and Literal Version by Raymond Garlick), Newtown, Gwasg Gregynog, 1985.

COLLECTED POEMS 1946–86, Llandysul, Gomer Press, 1987.

TRAVEL NOTES (New Poems), Llandysul, Gomer Press, 1992.

I AM DAVID (words by Raymond Garlick, music Mervyn Burtch, translation Eirian Davies), Carmarthen, Trinity College Publications, 1994.

Anthologies

POETRY FROM WALES, Poetry Book Monthly, Vol. 6, No. 5, 1954.

ANGLO-WELSH POETRY 1480–1980, Bridgend, Poetry Wales Press, 1984, revised 1993 (with Roland Mathias).

'A Preface to (contemporary) Anglo-Welsh Poetry', in NORTH DAKOTA QUARTERLY, 1989 (nineteen poets represented).

Prose

'The Golden Mountain' (short story), DOCK LEAVES 1, 1, Christmas 1949.

'Angharad and the Sphinx' (short story), DOCK LEAVES 1, 2, Easter 1950.

'The Words in My Life, Passages from an Autobiography', ANGLO-WELSH Review 13, 31, Summer 1963.

'A Short Walk in the Desert' in PLANET 4, 1971.

'The Good Tourist's Guide to the Courts', PLANET 12, June/July 1972.

In ARTISTS IN WALES 2, ed. Meic Stephens, Llandysul, Gomer Press, 1973.

'Fourth of May', ANGLO-WELSH REVIEW 62, 1978.

'English as a Language of Wales', QUEST 3, 1981.

In AUTHORS TAKE SIDES ON THE FALKLANDS, ed. Woolf and Wilson, London, Cecil Woolf, 1982.

'Easing the Tension' (interview by John Barnie), PLANET 62, 1987.

'Inspiration and Perspiration', POETRY WALES, 24, 1, 1988.

'A Poet Looks Back', BOOK NEWS, Summer 1989.

Interview (by David Lloyd), POETRY WALES 26, 3, January 1991.

'Choosing Wales', in DISCOVERING WELSHNESS, ed. Fiona Bowie and Oliver Davies, Llandysul, Gomer Press, 1992.

'Dock Leaves and Nettles', unpublished paper read to the colloquium (13 March 1993) at Gregynog of the University of Wales Association for Welsh Writing in English.

'A Small Boy in the Thirties, I', PLANET 102, December 1993.

'A Small Boy in the Thirties, II', PLANET 103, February 1994.

'A Small Boy in the Thirties, III', PLANET 104, April 1994.

'Portfolio', PLANET 107, October 1994.

'Some Painters', PLANET 108, December 1994.

'Dylan Thomas and Others', PLANET 109, February 1995.

'Mr Powys and Miss Playter', PLANET 110, April 1995.

Criticism

Editorials (twenty-six) in DOCK LEAVES/ANGLO-WELSH REVIEW, 1949–60.

'Anglo-Welsh Poetry from 1587 to 1800', THE DUBLIN MAGAZINE, January/March 1954.

'Seventy Anglo-Welsh Poets', THE WELSH ANVIL VI, December 1954.

'Anglo-Welsh Literature', Port Talbot, Alun Books, undated.

Debate with Harri Webb, POETRY WALES, vols. 2, 2 and 3, Summer/Winter 1966.

'Welsh Literature in English', NEW CATHOLIC ENCYCLOPEDIA, New York/St Louis, McGraw Hill, 1967.

'Is There an Anglo-Welsh Literature?', in LITERATURE IN CELTIC COUNTRIES, ed. J. E. Caerwyn Williams, Cardiff, University of Wales Press, 1971.

AN INTRODUCTION TO ANGLO-WELSH LITERATURE, Cardiff, University of Wales Press (Writers of Wales), 1970, revised 1972.

'On the Growing of DOCK LEAVES', PLANET 9, December 1971/January 1972.

'The Shapes of Thoughts', POETRY WALES 9, 2 (Dylan Thomas Special Issue), Autumn 1973.

'Publishing Anglo-Welsh Writers', BOOK NEWS, Spring 1980.

'Powys in Gwynedd', in ESSAYS ON JOHN COWPER POWYS, ed. Belinda Humfrey, Cardiff, University of Wales Press, 1972.

'Blaenau Remembered', in RECOLLECTIONS OF THE POWYS BROTHERS, ed. Belinda Humfrey, London, Peter Owen, 1980.

'Anglowalesisk litteratur', HORISONT, Denmark, 1980.

'Vale Atque Ave', NEW WELSH REVIEW 1, 1, Summer 1988.

Letters, Diaries etc.

In the National Library:

Correspondence with the following: Brenda Chamberlain, Redwood Anderson, Jacques Wirz of Basel (both sides, 1947–57/1985–93), A. G. Prys-Jones (1950–85), Cledwyn Hughes (1958–70), Elwyn Davies of Bunnick, the Netherlands.

Garlick's diary of his pilgrimage to Rome in 1950 and intermittent diaries up to 1986.

Note-books and worksheets from 1964.

Draft (1950) of AN INTRODUCTION TO ANGLO-WELSH LITERATURE.

A (mono) record (Argo PLP1156) exists containing twenty-one poems composed up to and including 1970. (Side 2 contains poems by John Ormond.)

An hour-long video interview, conducted by Meic Stephens, was made recently by the North Wales Arts Association. It has not, at the time of writing, yet been released.

CRITICISM ON RAYMOND GARLICK

Roland Mathias, review of A SENSE OF EUROPE, ANGLO-WELSH REVIEW 41, 1969.

Gerald Morgan, review of A SENSE OF EUROPE, POETRY WALES 4, 3.

John Hill, 'The Poetry of Raymond Garlick', ANGLO-WELSH REVIEW 47, 1972.

Jeremy Hooker, POETRY WALES 8, 4, 1973.

Tony Bianchi, 'Let the Poem Show Praise', PLANET 40, 1977.

Anthony Conran, POETRY WALES 12, 3, 1977 (review of INCENSE).

Glyn Jones and John Rowlands, PROFILES, Llandysul, Gomer Press, 1980.

Robert Minhinnick, 'Problem Class: Raymond Garlick and the Welsh', POETRY WALES 23, 2/3, 1988.

Tony Conran, 'An Abdication from Time', THE NEW WELSH REVIEW 1, 1, Summer 1988.

Leslie Norris, THE NEW WELSH REVIEW 1, 1, Summer 1988.

Megan Sue Lloyd, 'Texts against chaos: Anglo-Welsh identity in the poetry of R. S. Thomas, Raymond Garlick and Roland Mathias', Ph.D. thesis, University of Kentucky, 1992.

Tony Conran, ALL HALLOWS, Llandysul, Gomer Press, 1995 (the first 'movement' of this poem is devoted to Raymond Garlick and amounts to a critique of his life and work).

Acknowledgements

Raymond and I join in paying tribute to Trinity College, Carmarthen, and in particular to its English Department, in which we spent our happiest and most creative years. We pay special tribute to the memory of Keith Thomas and Tudor Bevan, whose tragically premature deaths robbed us of congenial colleagues and good friends.

In more than the usual sense, this essay could not have been written without the artist who forms its subject-matter. Raymond has given me unstintingly of his time, his assistance, his encouragement and his library and papers. I trust that I shall continue for a long time to enjoy the friendship that grew originally out of respect for the quality of his teaching and his professional integrity.

Meic Stephens has, as ever, been enormously helpful and encouraging.

My wife, Edna, by patiently listening to my reading aloud of the essay, has been more influential than she has realized.

The Author

Don Dale-Jones was born at Ruthin, Denbighshire, in 1935. After education at Cambridge and Nottingham universities, he taught at Nottingham and Rhyl, then worked for fifteen years as lecturer and senior lecturer in English at Trinity College, Carmarthen. In April 1979, he became the first Regional Official, Wales, of the National Association of Teachers in Further and Higher Education, a position from which ill-health obliged him to retire prematurely in 1987. He lives in Carmarthen and enjoys part-time teaching, editing, reviewing, writing and cultivating his garden.

He has edited TWELVE MODERN ANGLO-WELSH POETS, University of London Press, 1975; WALES TODAY, A COLLECTION OF POEMS AND PICTURES FOR CHILDREN, Gomer Press, 1976 (with Randal Jenkins); the COLLECTED POEMS OF T. HARRI JONES, Gomer Press, 1977, reprinted 1987 (with Julian Croft); and the COLLECTED POEMS OF A. G. PRYS-JONES, Gomer Press, 1988. He has written the WRITERS OF WALES monographs on EMLYN WILLIAMS (1979) and A. G. PRYS-JONES (1992).

Designed by Jeff Clements
Typeset at the University of Wales Press in
11pt Palatino and printed in Great Britain by Dinefwr
Press, Llandybïe, 1996

British Library Cataloguing in Publication Data.
A catalogue record for this book is available from the
British Library.

ISBN 0-7083-1322-1

The Publishers wish to acknowledge the financial
assistance of the Arts Council of Wales towards the cost
of producing this volume.